In the
Shadow
of the
Mountain

In the Shadow of the Mountain
The Spirit of the CCC

Edwin G. Hill

Washington State University Press
Pullman, Washington

Washington State University Press, Pullman, Washington 99164-5910

First published 1990
99 98 97 96 95 94 93 92 91 90   10 9 8 7 6 5 4 3 2 1

Printed and bound in the United States of America on pH neutral, acid-free paper

Library of Congress Cataloging-in-Publication Data:

Hill, Edwin G., 1919-
In the shadow of the mountain: the spirit of the CCC/by Edwin G. Hill.
p. cm.
Includes bibliographical references (p.) and index.
ISBN 0-87422-073-4 (alk. paper)

1. Civilian Conservation Corps (U.S.). 2. Youth—Employment—United States—History. 3. New Deal, 1933-1939. 4. Depressions—1929—United States. I. Title.
HD6273.H535 1990
333.7'2'0973—dc20   90-12576 CIP

Cover: CCC convoy on a mountain road in the western United States. *Manuscripts, Archives, and Special Collections, Washington State University Library, Pullman*

Table of Contents

Foreword by Craig Holstine   vii

Acknowledgments   ix

Introduction: FDR's Civilian Conservation Corps   xiii

—My Years in the CCC—

Chapter One   Before My Journey   1

Chapter Two   The Bottom Falls Out   15

Chapter Three   Camp Hard Labor Creek   23

Chapter Four   Long Trail West to Camp Sunset   35

Chapter Five   Camp Skamania and Mt. Adams   69

Chapter Six   Camp Cougar and Mt. St. Helens   89

—The CCC Story—

Chapter Seven   The CCC in the Pacific Northwest   97

Chapter Eight   Accomplishments Across the USA   135

Chapter Nine   Where Have the CCC Boys Gone?   153

Appendix One   Camp Soda Springs Behavior Book   169

Appendix Two   Barracks Writers   174

Appendix Three   History of Fort Lewis CCC District   177

Selected References   182

Index   183

Foreword

by Craig Holstine

The formation of the Civilian Conservation Corps in the early 1930s represented a massive renewal of Federal involvement in the thoughtful stewardship of our nation's natural resources—an obligation that had waned since the days of Theodore Roosevelt and Gifford Pinchot. An army of enthusiastic youths enlisted in the CCC, eager to do whatever tasks they were assigned. Their many accomplishments, so aptly described by Ed Hill, remain an important legacy in the decades-long struggle over conservation, a battle going on yet today.

In the Shadow of the Mountain, however, also tells us about how the CCC changed one man's life (Ed Hill's), as well as those of his fellow enrollees. Today, we hear again and again from CCC veterans about how the 3C's turned their lives around. Desperate young men in desperate times were given the chance to be gainfully employed, learn occupations, receive education, send money home, and to earn self respect and confidence in an era of social and economic chaos. Enlistment in the CCC may not have been a positive experience for every young man, but it appears to have been so for the vast majority.

Why was the Civilian Conservation Corps a good experience for these youths, working and living under semi-military control while earning $30 a month for doing hard, physical labor, often in locales far removed from their homes? It appears that the circumstances and difficult times of the early decades of the twentieth century forged a "type" of youth particularly suited to life in the CCC's. Since World War II, of course, peace and prosperity have produced new generations (to which I belong) generally unfamiliar with such hardships. Thus, it seems unlikely that a similar organization today would attract the devoted loyalty that the CCC did a half-century ago.

The CCC's accomplishments, however, have continued to influence succeeding generations. Those of us enjoying outdoor activities still make use of many facilities built by them: parks, campgrounds, bridges, hiking trails, forest roads, and the like. Agencies such as the U. S. Forest Service and the National Park Service continue to occupy structures erected by the 3C's, saving taxpayers the expense of constructing new, more costly quarters. CCC sponsored projects—reforestation, fire prevention, water conservation, historical restorations, and wildlife, wildlands, and wilderness protection—still continue to reap economic, social, and recreational benefits for society many decades later.

Several years ago I met Ed Hill in Yakima, Washington. As our conversation touched on mutual interests, a familiar story unfolded, one I had heard before from CCC veterans (and I was to hear again, at Ed's invitation, at CCC alumni picnics held under the pines by clear mountain streams). He said hard times and the lure of adventure had landed him in the CCC and far from home, his experiences as an enrollee had given him purpose and a sense of direction, and his time in the 3C's had been the high point of his life. Ed also confided that he had taken on the challenge of putting his memories on paper. His reverence for the CCC and his sense of mission greatly impressed me.

Now, seven years after his research and writing first began, *In the Shadow of the Mountain* has come to fruition, describing what life was like for an enrollee in the CCC in Georgia and the Pacific Northwest. With this book, we can thank Ed for his "We can take it" (an old CCC slogan) determination in keeping the "spirit" of the Civilian Conservation Corps alive for later generations to read about.

Cheney, Washington
June 29, 1990

Acknowledgments

It was one of the greatest things that ever happened in this country as far as I am concerned—the Civilian Conservation Corps, 1933-1942. My sincerest appreciation goes out to all of those people whose contributions helped to make *In the Shadow of the Mountain* possible.

I am especially grateful to Director Thomas H. Sanders of the WSU Press, to Editor Glen Lindeman for his interest and untiring efforts in the final preparation of the manuscript, and to the rest of the WSU Press staff for their kind assistance and excellent cooperation.

Friends from the Gifford Pinchot National Forest, the Wenatchee National Forest, and the National Association of Civilian Conservation Corps Alumni (including Marion Wilbur of the "Spirit of the CCC" San Diego Chapter #55, as well as members and officers of Yakima Valley Chapter #39) were very helpful in assisting me in my research. Also, many thanks to the CCC "boys," who provided essential information and stories about the Great Depression era and the Civilian Conservation Corps.

I owe great gratitude to my wife Velma, to my sons Ron and Ed (both of whom would have enjoyed a "hitch" in the 3C's if it could have been possible), and to my daughter Carole, whose "You can do it Dad" kept me at the task. Likewise, a special thanks to my granddaughters Angie and Lisa and daughter-in-law Bonnie for their help, and to my brother Allen and other family members across the country for their support and encouragement.

Finally, I am grateful to historian Craig Holstine of Archaeological and Historical Services at Eastern Washington University, without whose interest and help this book would not have been written. And, to Robert W. Larse (son of Camp Goldendale Superintendent Victor W. Larse), to Wapato High School teacher Coleman Burke, as well as to Judy Caughlan, teacher, CCC and Forest Service historian, and friend, who patiently assisted and inspired me along the way.

The CCC "We can take it" boys—and a *girl—who contributed to this work included: my cousin Julian Patrick, Fred Arnold, Donald Brown, George "Bud" Bush, William D. Cameron, Michael Crabtree, *Lillian Durbon, Edward Hayes, Ben Hoffman, Sam Keikkala, Edward Kelley, Melford Knight, Robert Kraner, Steve Kutchko, Paul A. Lawrence, Robert K. LeBeck, J. D. McReynolds, Orville Olney, A. G. StJohn, Joseph F. Schaffhauser, Sr., Myer Schaffner, Leonard Sherry, Robert Smith, Victor W. Snyder, William F. Spigelmyer, Clayton Strandberg, Daniel Szasz, Ralph C. Thomas, Jim Von Spacher, and John Wies.

Assisting from the U. S. Forest Service were the following: Chuck Frame, Mike Hiler, Barbara Hollenbeck, Bob Horn, Cheryl Mack, Jamie Tolfree, James L. Unterwegner, and Gerald W. Williams.

Wayne Eden of the Washington State Parks and Recreation Commission likewise proved to be most helpful.

Thank you one and all!

Edwin G. Hill
Wapato, Washington
May 16, 1990

Timberline Lodge at Mt. Hood, Oregon. This exceptional structure was one of thousands of new public works projects undertaken by the government during the New Deal era. *Boychuk Collection, Oregon Historical Society, Portland*

Introduction

FDR's Civilian Conservation Corps

In one of my conversations with the President in March 1933, he brought up the idea that became the Civilian Conservation Corps. Roosevelt loved trees and hated to see them cut and not replaced . . . He thought any man or boy would rejoice to leave the city and work in the woods.

Frances Perkins, Secretary of Labor

In the spring of 1933, during the darkest days of the Great Depression, there were 13,689,000 unemployed people in the United States according to an American Federation of Labor estimate. One wage earner out of four was without a job and had no hope of finding one.

More than a million hobos rode the rails on freight cars, and, according to the Children's Bureau, a quarter of a million of them were boys and girls—and there were many thousands more who hitchhiked about the country, all looking for jobs.

Living conditions were at an all time low: poor housing, not enough food, minimal health care, insufficient clothing—people living without hope! Even for those who were employed, millions were underpaid or worked only part time. In early 1933, families were losing their homes at the rate of more than a thousand a day—almost everyone suffered to some degree.

On July 2, 1932, as the Great Depression worsened, Franklin D. Roosevelt had become the Democratic Party's presidential candidate with these words: "I pledge you, I pledge myself, to a new deal for the American people."

Roosevelt was elected the thirty-second President of the United States, and took office on Sunday, March 4, 1933.

In his inaugural address, he brought new hope to the American people: "This great Nation will endure as it has endured, will revive and will prosper. So . . . let me assert my firm belief that the only thing we have to fear is fear itself . . . The people of the United States have not failed."

The New Deal

Roosevelt, after his landslide victory, felt confident that Congress and the American people would support him as he led the nation forward with the "New Deal." With conservation and unemployment problems being among FDR's prime concerns, one of his first proposals was to have a bill passed to create the Civilian Conservation Corps (CCC).

It would have two main purposes: (1) to provide employment for young men, who would be required to send money home to their needy families, and (2) to protect the nation's long neglected natural resources by using the enrollees to work on conservation projects.

Roosevelt believed that such a corps would be one of the key New Deal programs, helping to lead the nation out of its economic and social woes. Thus, Roosevelt had the foresight to see that, while preserving and upgrading the nation's natural and cultural resources, such as the forests, parks, wildlife refuges, farmlands, national monuments, historic sites, and beaches, the program also would save the nation's most precious attribute— the youth.

The idea of organizing young men for constructive work was not an entirely new one. In 1912, noted Harvard philosopher

William James wrote in an essay, titled "The Moral Equivalent of War," that destructive tendencies in young men might be turned to good purposes with conscription of the whole youthful population for peaceful service. Also, work armies were tried in Bulgaria, Germany, Austria, and other countries in the 1920s and 1930s, but these organizations usually were thwarted to paramilitary or political purposes.

In the United States, the time had come for such a program. Roosevelt later claimed he was unaware of William James's views and uninfluenced by events in Europe. Earlier, while part of the New York political scene, however, Roosevelt was involved with various state conservation and employment activities. Also, he was aware of other similar programs being conducted in other states. With support from his associates, the plan for the Civilian Conservation Corps had been conceived in the months before the inauguration.

On March 21, 1933, the newly elected president sent to the seventy-third Congress, then in emergency session, a proposal to recruit thousands of unemployed young men into a peacetime labor force.

Roosevelt stated: "I propose to create a civilian conservation corps to be used in simple work, not interfering with normal employment, and confining itself to forestry, the prevention of soil erosion, flood control and similar projects."

Congress moved swiftly. By March 31, 1933, the Emergency Conservation Work Act had passed both houses and was on the president's desk to be signed.

Executive Order 6101 Establishes the CCC Organization, April 5, 1933

FDR's insistence that work begin immediately was not taken lightly. The first enrollee, Henry Rich of Alexandria, Virginia, was inducted into the CCC on April 7, 1933. Only thirty-four days had passed since FDR's inauguration.

The first CCC camp, known as Camp Roosevelt, was formed on the George Washington National Forest near Luray, Virginia, on April 17, 1933.

Supervisors from the National Forest Service, the Soil Conservation Service, the National Park Service, and other federal and state agencies would direct the young men on projects during working hours, but, in the evenings and off duty hours, U. S. military personnel took charge of the enrollees at the barracks camps. The officers and enlisted men, however, had strict orders not to impose military training.

Most of the officers were Army reservists, but the Navy and Marine Corps provided cadre as well. George Dern, the Secretary of War, would later report at a cabinet meeting that the officers gained valuable experience in the CCC.

"They have had to learn," Dern stated, "to govern men by leadership, explanation, and diplomacy rather than discipline. That knowledge is priceless to the American Army."

Many of the reserve officers called up during the CCC mobilization were themselves out of work or underemployed. The reservists tended to be college educated, open minded, and not hidebound by military regulations—ideal attributes for directing companies of youths. A number of civilian doctors also began signing up to serve the boys in the camps. During the depression years, numerous MD's faced financial disaster since patients were unable to pay their bills. Many of the new civilian supervisors and foremen, or Local Experienced Men (LEM's), at the CCC camps likewise had been unemployed. It was these men—supervisors, camp officers, foremen, and doctors—who became the role models for the young enrollees.

In his message to Congress when proposing to create the Civilian Conservation Corps, Roosevelt had said, "I call your attention to the fact that this type of work is of definite, practical value, not only through the prevention of great present financial loss, but also as a means of creating future national wealth."

Enrollees had to be eighteen to twenty-five years of age, unemployed, unmarried, from families on "relief," and physically fit. They were to receive $30 monthly, plus food, shelter, clothing, and medical care. Each month, the government took $25 out of an enrollee's salary and mailed a check directly to the enlistee's home, to help his family and relatives get through the hard times.

The CCC boys would pick up their $5 (or at times, $8) spending money at the pay table toward the end of each month. A newly enlisted Army private at the time received only $18. This fact caused some disgruntlement. "Leaders" and "Assistant Leaders," usually selected from the Local Experienced Men, earned $45 and $36 respectively.

By April 10, 1933, the original quota of 25,000 youths had been filled, but the program continued to rapidly expand. By July 1, 1933, 1,300 CCC camps were constructed and filled with 274,375 enlistees, breaking all American peacetime mobilization records.

Before the CCC program ended nine years later, 3,000,000 men had served in the greatest conservation program ever undertaken by any nation. Most were white youths, but 200,000 Blacks, 225,000 World War I veterans, and thousands of Native Americans across the country and "Territorials" in Puerto Rico, Alaska, Hawaii, and the Virgin Islands also served.

No job was too big or too tough for the "We can take it" boys—the CCC.

MY YEARS IN THE CCC

CCC tent camp, Lassen National Forest, northern California. *Manuscripts, Archives, and Special Collections, Washington State University Library, Pullman*

Chapter One

BEFORE MY JOURNEY

*I was born in a farmhouse near Greensboro,
Georgia, in 1919. In those days, most of the
births in that part of the country were attended
by a midwife, not a doctor. I was one of the
lucky few, brought into this world with the help
of a real M.D.*

Ed Hill

I believe that the more we know about the Great Depression
of the 1930s, the better we can appreciate our country today
and the standard of living we now enjoy.

Following is a recollection of my memories of the depression era, my boyhood, family, and friends, and the conditions as they were before FDR's "New Deal" established the Civilian Conservation Corps. In this chapter, I only describe that part of my early life that I consider as background for the purpose of this book: to tell the story and legacy of the Civilian Conservation Corps.

I consider myself lucky to have been born into a poor, but loving, family. I was ten years old when the 1929 stock market "Crash" plunged our nation into the depths of the greatest and longest depression it has ever known. As I "grew up" at home and in the CCC—the "We can take it" boys—I learned the value of hard work, thrift, education, and patience, and to pursue every aspiration, even the seemingly impossible, with a positive attitude.

Learning the Three "R's"

I was the youngest of three children, with a sister nine years older and a brother seven years older. As a youngster, in those lean depression times, I always seemed to be hungry. Early on, I was nicknamed "Lick Skillet."

I attended country schools through the eighth grade. Going to school was not easy in those days. We walked more than a mile each way, packing a sack lunch through cold, rainy, and windy weather. The roads in north central Georgia, which sometimes were merely trails through the woods, were sticky with red clay when it rained and covered with red dust when dry. On the way to school from one of the many farmhouses we lived in, I had to cross over a creek on a footlog felled across the stream as a substitute for a bridge.

The school held classes just seven months out of the year, and only the most basic subjects were taught—the three "R's," history, and geography. I spent after school hours doing chores and studying. The school had two rooms and two teachers: one taught the first four grades, and the other served as principal and instructed the fifth through eighth graders.

The eighth grade boys kept the fire burning in the big potbellied stove in one room, while the fourth grade boys, with a little help from the teacher, kept the stove going in their room. Local men cut and hauled the firewood to school, where they stacked it neatly in a dry place. They also donated their time to make necessary repairs to the furniture and facilities.

Water was carried about a hundred yards from an open "dug" well to the water cooler, a container that held about four gallons with a spigot to disburse it. Each student had to furnish his or her drinking cup. Some cups were handmade by folding

a sheet of writing paper in such a way that it would hold water—
at least long enough to get water from the spigot to the lips.

The girls' outhouse, a two-holer, was about a hundred feet
from the school, hidden in the underbrush with only the path to
it visible. One Halloween night, the boys moved this outhouse
to a position slightly behind its trench, then camouflaged the
trench with grass and leaves. The next day, when the first girl took
the path to the toilet and plunged in up to her knees, some of the
boys hiding in the underbrush laughed heartily at the poor girl's
expense. Another mischievous prank we indulged in was the
smearing of a little sorghum molasses around the toilet seats and
watching the girls as they came back to the classroom pulling at
their sticky clothes.

Textbooks were not furnished by the state or school
district. Each family had to supply the children with their own.
Students took special care of these books, so they could be
handed down to younger brothers and sisters or sold for enough
money to buy primers for the next year.

I remember the school's first pencil sharpener. The teacher
asked each student from those families who could afford it to
donate five cents. When enough money was collected, a sharpener was purchased and installed on a corner of the teacher's
desk, where everyone took a turn at sharpening their pencil. Until
then, we had used pocket knives, so we were all excited about
this new piece of factory-made equipment. Later, some parents
objected to its use because it seemed to them that it too quickly
used up scarce and "hard to come by" pencils.

Physical education was unheard of in the country schools
of this era, but we played hard during recesses and lunch breaks,
sometimes inventing games or activities. We always got enough
exercise, weather permitting, but the school did not have a
gymnasium or shelter of any kind for indoor activities.

Teachers demanded and received respect from students,
and did not tolerate talking in class, "horsing around," or any
other distraction. Teachers were there to teach and the students
were there to learn! If anyone got out of line, teachers had the
authority (and used it) to punish pupils with a few well placed

hacks with a paddle, extra schoolwork, or "staying in" at recess or after school.

A high school was located in the "town school," but the majority of local youths was unable to attend. Due to the Great Depression, money was unavailable to purchase books, supplies, clothes, or provide for transportation. I was one of the unfortunate majority.

Country Summertime

Long summer months were spent working on the farm. Summer jobs were hard to find, and paid only fifty cents per day for ten to twelve hours of work. The long work hours, especially without a break, seemed like a day without end to a young person. We were glad for the weekends, holidays, or even rainstorms, anything that would give us time off for recreation—swimming in the ponds and streams, hunting, fishing, and square dancing.

One long, hot summer, I and a couple of boyhood chums—a black friend named Tim Jenkins and Nolan "Shack-Poke" Leach, both of whom lived on nearby farms—built a dam across a creek, and "skinny dipped" and sailed a leaky boat on the pond. It leaked, of course, because we had no boat constructing skills, especially with old lumber.

Sweet and juicy watermelons were readily available when in season. We hauled them to the pond, letting them cool in the water, sometimes overnight. Watermelons quenched our thirst and satisfied our hearty appetites. We also feasted on fish, blackberries, and muscadines, a kind of purple grape growing wild along the streams.

Seining in the streams for fish was great sport, and the most enjoyable way of fishing for me. It provided food for the table and a lot of action, much more so than fishing with a hook and line, especially with my Dad and his friends. Many times during the long Georgia summers, we would pack cooking utensils along and have a fish fry on the bank of the stream, cooking the day's catch and crunchy cornmeal hush puppies over an open fire.

On one occasion, a friend of Dad's taught me how to land an eel. Eels, of course, are so slippery that it is almost impossible to hold onto them with bare hands. One hot summer day, we were seining in a nearby creek, and on the first try caught several fish and one large eel.

Wes Greenway, my Dad's fishing partner, shouted above the roar of the water, "Hey Lick, let me show you how to land this eel."

Using a stick to demonstrate, he said to me: "You catch the eel about the middle of its body with your teeth and hold onto it. It will squirm and wiggle and try to escape, but you just hold on—the eel won't get away."

It is a sure way to land an eel, but just the thought of a slimy eel in my mouth always kept me from trying to land one in that manner.

Rural Life

Even though the work was hard, money was scarce, and we had none of the modern conveniences of today, life was good on the farm. Somehow, there was always time to sing along to a five string banjo, a guitar, or a fiddle. I performed on the guitar and violin, and my brother Howard Clayton Hill (known as "Clayton," or by his nickname, "Boots") played the harmonica, guitar, and banjo. We really enjoyed country music and formed a band, performing at weekly square dances in the community.

Local youths attending Friday evening dances let off steam by dancing and partying, or just by enjoying each other's company. We did not charge a fee for playing because most of the people were unemployed, but the square dance "caller" accepted small donations to help defray expenses. Problems seldom occurred, except when someone acquired a bottle of "moonshine" whiskey, also known as "white lightning," "mule kick," or "panther juice." For the most part, people were courteous and well-mannered.

From the time I learned to read, I never passed up an opportunity to read a book. One of my fondest memories is of my friend Fred Carlan and myself spending a day on a creek bank with western magazines and Zane Grey books, just reading and talking about the West, with time out for an occasional "skinny dip" in the creek to cool off in the hot weather—and to sneak a few smokes of "rabbit tobacco," a weed that grows wild in the South.

Most transportation was by buggy, wagon, or train, so it was slow traveling, especially for those who lived in rural areas. By moving along leisurely, however, we had time to observe the countryside: the farms, trees, fields, streams, wildlife, and the farmers working in the fields.

In those days, there were no freeways, few paved roads, and very few automobiles to travel on them. County roads were maintained by convicts housed in camps adjacent to the roadways. They labored from sunup to sundown, doing hand work. The only "motorized" equipment were the trucks transporting the prisoners and, perhaps, a road grader pulled by a tractor.

At the impressionable age of five or six, I first saw a convict camp closeup while passing by in a wagon with my uncle, Felix Patrick, and his sons, Julian and Elmer. My cousins and I were scared—we had heard frightening stories about "convicts"! The cells housing the prisoners were cages. Mounted on wheels, they had metal-bar sides, with a roof and an iron-bar door. Four Black men were locked in each cell, with barely enough room to move around, since the metal cots took up most of the space.

In summer heat or winter cold, convicts could be seen working with picks, shovels, and sledgehammers along the roadways, while a guard with a shotgun watched over them. Many were hobbled with chains on their ankles, allowing them to take only short steps. All were dressed in black and white striped pants and shirts of heavy cloth.

Prisoners began the day at sunup, with cornmeal mush for breakfast, cornmeal again with "sowbelly" at noon, and, at about sundown, cornbread, "sowbelly," vegetables, such as collard greens, and, if they were lucky, buttermilk.

The weekly visit to town was an all-day affair. We loaded the light wagon with fresh produce, mainly butter and milk from the dairy and eggs from the hen house. We looked forward to seeing the sights of town, visiting with friends and relatives, some of whom we had not seen in weeks, and enjoying a "store bought" ice cream cone or a small bag of penny candy. Some raisins or even a banana were real treats.

To a country boy, the town square with its courthouse of red brick and tall white columns, the vendors selling hot roasted peanuts, and even the horse watering trough were indeed sights to behold. There the people met to discuss the weather, politics, farming, and to "swap" fish stories.

My father, Henry, caught so many catfish from the Oconee River that his cronies called him "Catfish Hill." After he was forced to retire from work because of bad health, Dad spent almost every day, weather and health permitting, fishing in the nearby river and creeks.

His favorite method of fishing was with a "trotline." It consisted of a main line strung along or across streams, to which other lines with hooks were attached at intervals. Using a "trotline," he set lines and baited hooks early in the morning, checked them at intervals during the day, and returned home in the afternoon with the catch, or left the lines overnight and visited them the next day.

The highlight of the year came in the fall when cotton, the area's cash crop, was picked and readied to be ginned. Cotton picking machines had not been invented yet, so the crop was handpicked, then loaded onto wagons with high sideboards, and pulled out of the fields by a team of horses or mules.

Riding high up on top of the wagon as it made its way to the cotton gin in town was a great treat. After arriving at the gin, we waited in line for several hours for our cotton to be ginned. These were happy hours spent anticipating the treats that would be purchased with some of the cash from the sale of the cotton.

The Shiloh Baptist Church "down at the crossroads," which my family attended, was a small congregation established in 1795 when George Washington was president. The land on which it stood was donated by a plantation owner for the purpose of establishing both a church and a public school. A church was built there along with a school, and weekly services have been held continuously ever since. The educational program at the church, its religious ideals and training, and the social activities, gave strength, character, and a lifetime of direction to its members.

The church and school stood adjacent to an open playground, used by both institutions. The public school teacher usually taught Sunday school as well. My mother, Deuella, was the church pianist, while Dad served as a deacon.

Every Christmas and Thanksgiving, children were organized to present holiday programs, which were looked forward to with much excitement. Even during the worst of the depression, parents usually managed to prepare Thanksgiving and Christmas dinners with gifts and treats for their families.

Located as it was in a rural district, the church was a popular gathering place, at times overflowing with so many people that they all could not get in. Day-long services with a picnic on the grounds, and a "homecoming" held one Sunday every year, always drew folks from surrounding communities.

Even though expenses were cut to the barest minimum in operating the church, financial problems persisted during the depression years, and at times proved almost impossible to cope with, despite the reduction of the pastor's salary to just five dollars a week. Firewood, however, was furnished at no cost, and the building repairs and grounds upkeep were done by members of the congregation, many of whom were themselves unemployed or only working part time.

The church did not have a baptistry, or even plumbing, so baptismal services were conducted at a nearby creek. Alongside the little stream, a small pool was constructed with a little ditch leading into it. I was baptized in this "outside" baptistry when I was twelve years old.

The pastor once said jokingly, "I've baptized so many converts in this creek that I know every crawdad and tadpole here by their first name."

The present Shiloh Baptist Church is only the third building occupied by the congregation since 1795. It stands about a mile from the site of the original church. The first church was destroyed by fire, and the second one, located only a few hundred feet from the present building, was destroyed by a tornado before it was finished.

Hard Times

My father moved us into town in 1924, seeking new employment opportunities and a better life, but without success. Living in town was an unfavorable experience for us. We were unaccustomed to the crowded conditions: large schools and churches, noisy traffic, and the nearby railroad yards. We occupied a little house with only a small yard, and our neighbors were just a few feet away.

Nor were we any better off financially. My father found only part-time work in the local sawmill, not earning enough money to provide the minimum necessities for a family of five. To make matters worse, we missed our old friends back in the country. We were unhappy and disappointed, so we moved back to a farm after living in town for a little more than a year.

When the "Big Crash" came in 1929, I was a ten year old attending the grade school about two miles from home. Being a farm boy, of course, I was unaccustomed to modern conveniences. Our old farmhouse had fireplaces for heating, a wood-burning range for cooking, and kerosene lamps for lighting. There was no electricity. In those days, in fact, only about one out of every fifty farms had electricity. Water was carried in buckets about two hundred yards from a spring that also served as a cooler for perishable foodstuff.

In addition to our economic difficulties, my mother's failing health contributed to our hardships. She had been frail for several years, suffering from pellagra, a disease caused by a deficiency of niacin in the diet, but the illness she now contracted was different.

At the onset, it became difficult for her to swallow. Her condition gradually deteriorated, until she could only take in liquids. Our family doctor sent her from one specialist to another, attempting to have her condition diagnosed. Eventually, she went to an Atlanta hospital to undergo medical evaluations and treatments. She finally was placed in a hospital in Sandersville, Georgia, but her health continued to deteriorate. After several weeks in this hospital, she was sent home, where she died a few days later. The year was 1935.

Left behind were my father, a married daughter, my brother, and myself, aged sixteen. We had been a close and happy family that had done everything together—played together, shared moments of joy or sorrow together, even gathered around the old pump organ to sing as my mother played and led the songs. She had taught my sister Henriella (her name was derived from combining my father's name "Henry" with my mother's name "Ella") to play the piano and organ. When sickness prevented my mother from serving as the church pianist, my sister substituted in her place.

Mother's death was a great loss to me and, of course, a tragedy for the entire family, especially because we had always been so close and caring. It was a time when I needed her understanding, love, and guidance, so her untimely death at only forty-five years of age left a vacancy in my life that could never be filled. The emptiness felt in the home far outweighed the hardships brought on by the depression or by the hospital and doctor expenses that wiped out the family assets.

We were not only in the depths of the Great Depression, but now we also were in the darkest days of a family in disarray, with no hope for the future. The loss was not only felt at home, but was sadly shared by the community and the church she had devoted her life to in loving service. I have a letter she wrote a short time before her death, in which she expressed concern that someone might forget to take their turn at cleaning the chapel before the Sunday services.

She always had been ready to help the sick and needy, and to give encouragement to those who needed it. A talented musician, she taught anyone wanting to learn, even giving lessons free of charge to those who were unable to pay.

Two years afterward, Father remarried. Then, several years later, with his new wife, Bessie, and their young son, Allen, he settled in Greensboro, the seat of the county where he had lived for most of his adult life.

He was known in the community for being liberal regarding "race" in an era when it was not popular, and he was noted for his compassion for people, regardless of who they were. He always counseled and helped in any way he could. He doctored sick animals, shared food with those in need, sat up with ill neighbors all night, and gave a helping hand to friends with their chores.

The need was never too big or too small to get his attention and help. Across the street from his house stood a church for local Black residents that he had helped build. A sign on it proclaimed:

HILL CHAPEL
BAPTIST CHURCH
Greensboro, Georgia

Mother's death was a major event in my life. It took away the security of a stable home environment and influenced me very much in my decision to join the Civilian Conservation Corps. Eight and a half months after she passed away, I enlisted in the CCC, where I hoped to find companionship and security, as well as a means of support.

I was not disappointed. The structured life of the CCC filled a very personal need in my life, providing a sense of belonging to a "home" again. It gave me inspiration, and an opportunity to learn—a chance to pause in those young and difficult years and decide what I wanted to do with my life.

I spent three years in the CCC: one year (July 9, 1936, to May 17, 1937) in Company 3442 at Camp Hard Labor Creek, SP-11, near Rutledge, Georgia; and two years (January 8, 1938, to December 21, 1939) with Company 5481 in the state of Washington at Camp Sunset Falls, F-39, near Yacolt. In this latter period, I also served in "summer camps" at Twin Buttes and Smokey

Creek, located in the Mt. Adams area north of Trout Lake, and at Cougar, a "side camp" near Mt. St. Helens.

The three years I served in the Civilian Conservation Corps were the most enjoyable and rewarding of my life.

"Hooverville" in the Connecticut Avenue vicinity on the Seattle waterfront, about 1934. *Washington State Library, Olympia*

Chapter Two

THE BOTTOM FALLS OUT

*How I wish I could cheer up the poor old
President* [Herbert Hoover].

Secretary of State Henry L. Stimson, 1930

T here are many opinions about the causes of the Great Depression. In this short chapter, I present my understanding of these events, based on my personal experiences in those hard times and on my own study of this phase of our national history.

For a variety of reasons, boom and bust business cycles have been common in America's past. No previous economic downturn, however, equalled the Great Depression of the late 1920s and 1930s for severity and universal hardship.

The prevailing view of many is that the depression had its roots in World War I (1914-1918). Due to the exigencies of making war, the European powers engaged in the conflict had focused their manpower and industrial production on the promotion of the war effort. Consequently, they could not produce enough foodstuffs or other basic commodities to adequately feed and maintain their armed forces or the civilian population.

As a result, the American agriculture and industrial sectors were called upon to fulfill the needs of the European Allies, particularly after the United States entered the conflict in 1917. Across the country, farms and factories greatly stepped up production of foodstuffs, supplies, and war equipment, and this great boom period for American agriculture and manufacturing continued for several years after the signing of the Armistice in 1918.

In the 1920s, however, as Europe regained much of its pre-war level of agricultural and industrial production, the demand for American food and manufactured products began slumping, resulting in huge surpluses flooding the U. S. marketplace. These surpluses, in turn, were destined to create a domino effect throughout the economy by the late 1920s and early 1930s. Industries and businesses, hampered by overstocked warehouses and insufficient sales to maintain profits, were forced to close down facilities and lay off workers.

The layoffs in turn meant that the amount of purchasing power available in the domestic sector declined—families had less money to buy goods, resulting in even greater surpluses. This was exacerbated by the fact that a high percentage, far higher than today, of the national wealth was concentrated in the hands of the well-to-do (people in the top five percent income group received one-third of the country's personal income). A majority of Americans, at that time, lived on very modest incomes indeed. As the vicious cycle of overproduction gained momentum and people did not have the money to buy goods, more factories were shut down and agricultural prices plummeted.

Economic prosperity did maintain some momentum during the "Roaring Twenties," but the roots of the coming depression already were planted. Farmers felt it first. At each harvest, agricultural surpluses grew, resulting in overflowing warehouses or grain elevators and, of course, very low prices.

With overproduction of cotton in the South, too much corn in the Midwest, and surpluses of wheat in the West, rural economic conditions grew worse. Farm families could not afford to purchase needed equipment and supplies. As conditions continued spiraling downward in the 1920s, much of the rural population, including my family, began to shift from the farms to the towns and cities seeking employment. Eventually, as a result of the depression, a fourth of the farmers in the United States lost their farms.

The Stock Market Crash

During the autumn of 1929, events unfolding at the New York stock exchange triggered the nationwide economic collapse that occurred in the financial and industrial sectors in the following months. On Monday, October 21, 1929, the selling of stock was heavy on Wall Street, and, in the following days, the market continued to falter. On "Black Thursday," October 24, 1929, an even greater selling wave occurred as nearly thirteen million shares were put on the block.

The "Big Crash" came on Tuesday, October 29! Stock prices plummeted precipitously when investors panicked, selling more than sixteen million shares. Investment losses on that day were fantastic—estimated at between eight and nine billion dollars—and the decline continued in the following weeks. By mid November, stock losses totalled at least thirty billion dollars, if not more, which was almost twice the amount of the national debt at that time, and nearly equaled the cost of America's participation in World War I.

Every person in the United States would feel the effects of the stock market plunge for many years to come as the nation slid into an ever deepening economic depression after 1929. Across the United States, businessmen, neighbors, and citizen groups congregated to discuss the crash. Landowners everywhere expressed fears of losing their property because of the spreading panic. At least one farm owner in our community committed suicide.

Hoover Days

Believing in a restricted role for government in regard to economic affairs, President Herbert Hoover instituted ineffective programs, which proved powerless to stem the chaotic economic and social conditions brought on by the stock market crash. The Hoover administration generally expected that the national marketplace eventually would correct itself, and good times would return. The president could not foresee that massive amounts of government involvement and money needed to be invested in innovative new social and economic programs to get unemployed and destitute people back on their feet, and to get factories running again.

Americans, however, doubted that Hoover even knew what he was talking about when he said, "prosperity is just around the corner."

This period of time, 1929 to 1932, came to be called "Hoover days." Poor and hungry people in the West and Southwest caught jackrabbits, calling them "Hoover-hogs." A common saying in the South was that if a cottontail ran across the road there were at least three hungry men trying to catch it. From New York to Seattle and from Florida to California, many of the jobless lived in makeshift "shanty towns" built of tar paper, scrap lumber, and packing crates, cynically named "Hoovervilles."

Economic collapse also spread throughout Europe and much of the rest of the world, contributing to worsening conditions in the United States, especially after 1931. By 1932, more than a million hobos rode the rails on freight cars that they called "Hoover Pullmans," in mockery of the Pullman cars used by the nation's first-class passengers. Many others hitchhiked about the country looking for jobs.

My friends and I never "rode the rails," but we did a lot of hitchhiking around Georgia for the same reason so many others did—looking for work.

President Hoover was familiar with government food distribution programs. When the United States had entered World War I, he was appointed director of the Food Administration, helping to organize a national program of food conservation. He also had guided the Commission for Belgium Relief, the greatest relief program of the World War I era, and was honored as a "great humanitarian" for his efforts.

But in 1930, the president's newly created Emergency Relief Organization was ineffective. Established to coordinate philanthropic and private donations to local relief organizations on a national scale, it did not receive the necessary voluntary funds and support to provide even the barest essentials to needy people. The belief in voluntary involvement by citizens and a limited role for government remained central to Hoover's plans.

Equally ineffective was Hoover's "Give-A-Job" campaign of 1931. Homeowners were urged to provide a few hours of work to the unemployed by giving them odd jobs around the house.

As one person said, however, "Private philanthropy was virtually bankrupt in the face of great disaster."

Nothing the president did seemed to have any effect. Across the country, there was much talk and theorizing, but no one knew for certain why it was that the nation was steadily plunging into social and economic shambles. Hoover urged state and local governments to assume the responsibility for providing relief to needy people, but state and local resources were equally inadequate for maintaining effective food and employment programs.

When the morale of the people was at an all time low, Hoover said, "What this country needs is a great poem. Something to lift the people out of fear and selfishness."

By March 1933, at the end of Hoover's term in office, there were 13,689,000 unemployed in the United States, but unofficial figures went as high as 15,000,000. The First Baptist Church in El Paso, Texas, arranged to accept IOU's in the collection plate, and a Milwaukee Presbyterian Church provided free gasoline to needy parishioners.

States and municipalities rapidly were running out of funds, especially for relief programs. Some could provide only three cents or less per person for a meal. The Red Cross did what it could, but in some locations it could give families only seventy-five cents a week for food.

In the winter on the Great Plains, farmers burned "old corn" (corn held over from the crop a year earlier), since it sold for only $1.40 a ton whereas coal cost $4.00 per ton. It was cheaper to burn corn than buy coal.

In November 1932, in the darkest days of the Great Depression, eyes were turned toward the Democratic Party to find a solution to the country's ever worsening economic and social problems. At this time, the Governor of New York, Franklin D. Roosevelt, was selected as the Democratic presidential candidate. Here was an appealing public figure, who rekindled hope among the American people. FDR, whose campaign jingle was *Happy Days Are Here Again,* won by a "landslide" over Hoover.

Roosevelt's philosophy of direct and extensive government action inspired confidence in a people who had reached the bottom of despair. The depression had yet to run its course for years to come, but the long overdue social and economic reforms instituted by the Roosevelt administration paved the way for eventual recovery and the development of modern America. The Civilian Conservation Corps, always popular with the public, played a significant role in this process.

President Franklin D. Roosevelt, on first inspection tour of CCC camps, visits the "overhead" and enrollees of Company 350, Big Meadow Camp, Shenandoah National Park, Virginia, on August 12, 1933. The CCC weekly newspaper, *Happy Days*, reported that FDR was accompanied by CCC Director Fechner, Presidential Secretary Colonel Howe, Secretary of Agriculture Wallace, Secretary of Interior Ickes, the Forest Service's Major Stuart, NPS Director Cammerer, Third Corps Commander General Malone, American Federation of Labor President Green, and other invited guests and associates. *Manuscripts, Archives, and Special Collections, Washington State University Library, Pullman*

Chapter Three

CAMP HARD LABOR CREEK

*I wish I could spend a couple of months here
myself. The only difference between us is that I
am told you men have put on an average of 12
pounds each. I am trying to lose 12 pounds . . .
I have seen the boys themselves, and all you
have to do is look at them to see that the camps
are a success.*

FDR at Big Meadow Camp,
Shenandoah National Park,
August 12, 1933

I began my first CCC enrollment on July 9, 1936, at Hard Labor
Creek State Park, SP-11, near Rutledge, Georgia, about thirty
miles from home. Reportedly, the creek was named in
bygone days by slaves who found the bottomlands along it very
hot and difficult to farm because of swamps and marshes.

The oath that I was required to take upon entry into the
Civilian Conservation Corps was as follows:

I, _____, do solemnly swear (or affirm) that the information given above as to my status is correct. I agree to remain in the Civilian Conservation Corps for the period terminating at the discretion of the United States between ...., unless sooner released by proper authority, and that I will obey those in authority and observe all the rules and regulations thereof to the best of my ability and will accept such allowances as may be provided pursuant to law and regulations promulgated pursuant thereto. I understand and agree that any injury received or disease contracted by me while a member of the Civilian Conservation Corps cannot be made the basis of any claim against the Government, except such as I may be entitled to under the Act of September 7, 1916 (39 Stat. 742) (an act to provide compensation for employees of the United States suffering injuries while in the performance of their duties and for other purposes), and that I shall not be entitled to any allowances upon release from camp, except transportation in kind to the place at which I was accepted for enrollment. I understand further that any articles issued to me by the United States Government for use while a member of the Civilian Conservation Corps are, and remain, property of the United States Government and that willful destruction, loss, sale, or disposal of such property renders me financially responsible for the cost thereof and liable to trial in the civil courts. I understand further that any infraction of the rules or regulations of the Civilian Conservation Corps renders me liable to expulsion therefrom. So help me God.

The CCC was only three years old, but it already was credited with "doing the impossible," a reputation that would be remembered for years to come. How I wanted to be a part of all this! My brother, "Boots," already had served his enrollment in camps near Robertstown and Blue Ridge, Georgia. I had listened to his stories about the fun, work, and adventure of being in the CCC.

An especially interesting experience he told me about was the cleaning up and guard duty performed by his unit in Gainesville, Georgia, after the town was almost destroyed by a tornado. CCC boys helped clear the debris, and patrolled the streets to discourage plundering.

Other boys serving in the CCC came home for weekends, talking about camp life, the interesting things they did, their new clothes, and the great food served in the mess halls. They mentioned the fun they were having, and told me about the many skills they were learning, giving them faith in the future when there had been none before. With the lowering of the enlistment age to seventeen, I now was able to enroll. (The upper age limit for enlistment also changed in these years, fluctuating between twenty-three and twenty-eight.)

I, along with several boys from the community, including my cousin Julian Patrick, joined the CCC at Macon, Georgia, and were transported to a camp at Hard Labor Creek State Park, where we began our service. On our arrival, a group of young men met us as was the custom, calling out "fresh meat," "rookies," "you'll be sorry," and other unprintable remarks. The wisecracks were intended to be all in fun, but, at the same time, to scare the "new boys." After the initial greeting, we talked about the work, food, camp life, and the medical attention—the latter of which was described as consisting of "shots with long dull needles," and the issuing of bitter medicines and Paul Bunyan sized pills.

For me, it was the first time away from the home, family, and friends I had grown up with. All that was behind me now. I was in an unfamiliar situation with people I did not know. I was thankful, at least, that my cousin was in the same camp, for he was someone I had known, gone to school with, and played with as a child—someone I knew and trusted. We managed to get assigned to the same barracks and bunked side by side. It was much easier for me the first few nights in camp knowing that he was in the bed next to mine.

After reporting in, we were issued clothing, as well as two pair of "GI" shoes and such personal items as a razor, towels, bedding, toothbrushes, and a small stainless steel mirror. After a tour of the camp, including the mess hall where we ate our first CCC meal, we were free to shower and get better acquainted with the boys with whom we would be working and living.

There were two CCC camps—one on each side of Hard Labor Creek. The first one that had been established there was State Park CCC Camp SP-8, on the south side of the creek, known as "old camp." State Park CCC Camp SP-11, on the north side of the stream, was the more recent. It was there that I was assigned. The structures were new, and I was impressed by the well kept facilities and grounds, and by their orderly arrangement. There were four barracks, a mess hall and kitchen, officers' quarters, camp commander's and park superintendent's offices, a tool and equipment building, a supply and infirmary, and a recreation building, which was used as a classroom when necessary.

The camp was situated in a beautiful spot in the pines, approximately two miles north of Rutledge, Georgia. Camp SP-11, my new home, was the farthest from town. The road from town first passed the "old camp," crossed the creek on a bridge, and continued upstream a short distance to my camp.

Our primary purpose was to construct an earthen dam across Hard Labor Creek, and to clear the land behind it for a man-made lake. Cleaning out the stream bed below the dam site also was included in our tasks.

Another important duty was to build small check dams on the farms in the area, to help control erosion and reclaim cropland that had been damaged by years of raising cotton and corn. The small check dams consisted of rocks and wire, and stood across small gullies and other runoff channels to stop the soil from washing away. Seeding and transplanting grass also were a part of the soil reclamation program.

Barracks Life

At the camp, each enrollee did his share of window cleaning, mopping floors, "KP" (kitchen police), and keeping his own space in the barracks clean and tidy. Clothes and personal items were arranged in lockers according to prescribed regulations. I learned how to sew on a button, as well as how to launder and press clothes. All of the supplies and equipment needed to maintain the buildings and grounds, and for housekeeping chores, were supplied by the CCC, including washing machines for laundering.

Having access to Maytag wringer-type washing machines was something new for many of the boys, including myself. We kept them going evenings and weekends washing clothes. I enjoyed utilizing all the appliances and conveniences made possible with modern electrical hookups. Here we could listen to the radio without needing a battery for power, and spend our time in the barracks in the glow of electric lights, rather than the kerosene lamps that most of us had at home.

We worked forty hours during the week. On Saturday mornings, we cleaned the buildings and grounds in preparation for an inspection at noon, after which time we were free to do as we pleased for the remainder of the weekend; provided, of course, that everything was found to be satisfactory. In addition to Saturday noon passes, the men could, with the exception of those on weekend duty, apply for leave from Friday evening until work time Monday morning, on a rotation basis. A specified number of enrollees were kept in camp on weekends, however, when there was a threat of fires, floods, tornadoes, or other impending emergencies.

CCC trucks provided transportation to Madison, Georgia, the county seat. Madison was famous for being spared by General Sherman's Union army during the 1864-1865 "march" through the Confederacy in the latter days of the Civil War. Madison yet retained the beautiful columned homes of its antebellum days, when it was known as the most cultured and aristocratic town on the Charleston to New Orleans stagecoach route. The town was a special attraction to the CCC boys, who went there for entertainment, sight-seeing, and to mingle with the friendly residents.

I went home many weekends when off duty, and had the opportunity to play the fiddle or guitar at the square dances in my old hometown. I hitchhiked from Madison if I could not get a ride with one of the boys going my way. Before my six month enrollment was up, I bought my first automobile, a 1929 Chevrolet, with some help from my CCC pay sent home each month by the government. Although it was against the rules to have an automobile at camp, several enrollees kept them hidden in nearby pine thickets. By pooling our cash, we often shared the cost of gas, and rode together in one car to save money.

Much of our spare time in camp was spent writing letters, reading, playing musical instruments, or hiking near the camp or along the creek. No alcohol or drugs were allowed, but now and then "moonshine" whiskey was sneaked in. If discovered by the cadre, stiff punishment was imposed on offenders. Extra work details, restricted recreational privileges, or other disciplinary actions could be ordered by the commanding officer.

One weekend, while I was on KP duty, someone entered the kitchen supply room and "swiped" a few bottles of lemon extract, which has a considerable alcohol content. A couple of enrollees then drank it, going on a spree. The missing extract was reported to the officer in charge, who, while investigating the incident, confined the entire company to camp, except for work crews and persons on emergency leave.

The guilty men remained unknown and at large. Restrictions were in effect only a few days, including through a weekend, however, before the company became angry because of its confinement. The enrollees rooted out the culprits, and, after a "kangaroo court," reported them to the commanding officer, who dealt out adequate punishment.

Located a few miles from camp was a place called "Possum Hollow," where a solitary farmhouse with outbuildings stood in the remote countryside. Here lived a family that illegally distilled and sold whiskey. As already mentioned, contraband liquor was known by various colorful names—"moonshine" (because it was made by the light of the moon), "white lightning" (that is how it hit a person), and "panther juice" or "mule kick" (two apt descriptions). The concoction made by this family was reported to be a powerful substance well deserving of those nicknames, and Possum Hollow was notorious for wild binges.

It was off limits to CCC boys by order of the company commander, but several of the fellows went there anyway, in secrecy, of course. One day, a buddy and I decided to go ourselves, to see if everything we had heard was true, and what it would be like to rub shoulders with a moonshiner and his merchandise. We sure found out!

When we arrived, a rowdy gathering was in progress—men and women guzzling moonshine, singing drunkenly, laughing up a storm, and dancing riotously. The party was well underway! We watched for only a few minutes, our eyes wide open, when two men started a drunken argument. We never did know what they were arguing about, and it is doubtful that they did either. In a split second, fists were swinging and jabbing, a real fight was on, and it spread like wildfire through the crowd, immediately erupting into a brawl.

We knew what we had to do if we wanted to stay in the 3C's! Somehow managing to duck flying fists and bodies in the free-for-all, we beat it out of there and headed back to camp. We had found out more than we wanted to about Possum Hollow. It goes without saying that we never went back there again.

Working Hard in the CCC

At Camp Hard Labor Creek, I was assigned to a crew of workmen under the supervision of a park service foreman named Smith. He directed the Herculean task of clearing the creek bed of logs and brush that had accumulated over the centuries, clogging it and preventing the water from flowing freely. Brawn and hand tools—crosscut saws, axes, shovels, brush hooks, and picks—were necessary to accomplish the task. There was no power equipment.

We sawed and chopped logs, cut brush, and removed stumps. Many of the logs had been covered with water and muck for a very long time, and were waterlogged and extremely heavy. After digging and prying them loose, we sawed or chopped the logs into sections ten to twenty feet long, then manhandled them out of the stream.

This feat was accomplished by maneuvering the logs into a position where long, wooden poles could be placed under them. As many as five or six poles often were needed on a log, with men at the end of each pole lifting together. When cleared, the open creek channel allowed water to flow unobstructed downstream, thus minimizing the danger of floodwaters backing up and inundating nearby bottomland.

Working cooperatively was the only way the task could be accomplished, as it was heavy, strenuous work requiring much muscle power and coordination. We were issued hip boots, but, with our splashing around or stepping into water that came up over the tops, we often got wet anyway.

The area was infested with vermin and snakes in the hot summer months, adding to the misery of the work. Most of these "creeping things" were nonpoisonous, and no one was ever seriously infected or bitten, largely due to safety precautions taught and practiced in the CCC. Occasionally, a snake fell from a tree, landing on one of the boys.

Once, a snake somehow found its way into my rubber boot. As I frantically tried to get it out, I fell in the creek, but still managed to shuck the boot off in record time. It all happened so fast that I could not remember how I did it. I am sure the snake was as scared as I was.

Another time, a small snake dropping from some scrub brush went down the collar of one of the boys. I have never seen anyone remove a shirt so quickly. So fast it looked like one single movement—shirt off and snake free! In moments like these, it was little comfort to know that snakes and other residents of the wild probably are more afraid of humans than we are of them. Creek clearing, though, had a fringe benefit. It was much cooler working in or near water on hot sultry days, than it was on other projects where there was no stream close by to jump into.

"Another day another dollar" aptly described work in the CCC. The rewards from my first enlistment were many. I learned how to coexist with people, to cooperate within a group in achieving common goals, and to understand and respect the rights and opinions of others. I am grateful that I had the chance to learn these skills, and I feel that they remain with me still.

When the weather was too cold for working in the creek, I usually was assigned to an erosion control crew. It was interesting to learn how to build the small rock dams (called the "dam things" by the CCC boys), but I missed the excitement and adventure of clearing the creek, and always was ready and anxious to return to it.

Dinnertime

Food in the CCC generally was excellent. My first meal in a 3C's mess hall was a memorable one for a depression kid to whom food was dear. I ate enough for three men. There were eight of us seated at a table, family style. As soon as a dish or platter was emptied, it was refilled again until we had eaten as much as we wanted.

I was amazed at the variety and amount of food placed on a table for eight men to consume. In those lean years, I had not known such food existed! And, that first meal was typical: braised sirloin tips, vegetables, including tomatoes and potatoes, Waldorf salad, apples and nuts, bread and butter, orange marmalade, and ice cream for dessert.

The diet was calculated to supply the necessary minerals and vitamins for a healthy body, and was prepared by capable CCC cooks under the watchful eyes of a mess sergeant, usually an enrollee especially trained for that duty.

A former mess sergeant recalled, "I fed each man on thirty-nine cents a day; we didn't throw anything away."

The structured life-style of the CCC—work, sleep, exercise, and fresh air—gave us tremendous appetites. For the first time in our lives, we had all of the food we could want.

In fact, a 1940 Federal Security Agency study later reported, "The average enrollee gained more than eight pounds during his first six months, attributed to regular hours, healthful surroundings, good food and living conditions and proper medical and dental care."

Returning, Forty-eight Years Later

I visited Hard Labor Creek in the summer of 1985 for the first time since leaving in 1937—a journey into nostalgia. Standing on the bridge across the creek below the earthen dam, I reflected on my time spent there—the circumstances that had brought about my joining the CCC, the friends I had made, the work we did, my adventures, and the many positive ways in which the 3C's affected my life.

Our dam is there, holding back the waters of 275 acre Lake Rutledge. Hard Labor Creek flows freely in the channel we cleared. Many other fine state parks were built in Georgia by the CCC, but the park at Hard Labor Creek remains the largest and one of the most popular in Georgia. Its 5,800 acres, including the two lakes, Rutledge and Brantley, offer a wide variety of outdoor activities, including horseback riding, camping, swimming, fishing, and golf.

All evidence of my old camp, SP-11, has vanished. In its place now are the cabins and structures of Camp Rutledge, standing on the shoreline of the lake we created. I wondered if lumber from any of the old CCC buildings remained concealed within the walls of the nicely painted structures of the new group camp.

Remnants of the other camp, SP-8, still stand on the other side of the lake. Its buildings are empty, with just a few used as storage facilities. All of the structures need repairs. I gazed at them across the water, feeling a kinship to those old ghosts of a mighty fine past.

My First CCC Discharge

Camp Hard Labor Creek was the gateway to a new life and new experiences. I appreciated the good food and clothes, and enjoyed the companionship of 200 men my age. Before enlisting, all of us had been burdened with the same Great Depression hopelessness of a life without jobs and income. Obviously, we were thankful for the $5 spending money we received each month, and for the $25 monthly allotment sent home to help our families through those lean years.

I look back with great pride and satisfaction at the work accomplished and the fun I had in the year that I was stationed at Hard Labor Creek State Park.

The CCC placed limitations on the number of enlistments that enrollees could consecutively serve, and granted early discharges to boys finding work on the outside. Therefore, on May 17, 1937, during my second six month enlistment, I was granted a discharge to accept employment driving a lumber truck at a planing mill in Greensboro. (Eventually, multiple enlistments of more than a year were allowed—next time I would serve four six month "hitches.")

For now, I was back home "driving truck." In a few months, according to the usual Great Depression litany, business slowed, the plant curtailed operations, again I was unemployed.

And, I could find no other work!

Though I enjoyed being at home again for awhile with my relatives and friends, I missed being in the CCC, and I wanted to travel and seek new experiences. According to federal regulations at the time, I could re-enlist in the CCC after six months had passed since my discharge from Camp Hard Labor Creek.

This time I was given my choice of where to go in the United States, and I made the most of it!

North side of Mt. St. Helens, circa 1905. *Ashford Collection, Oregon Historical Society, Portland*

Chapter Four

LONG TRAIL WEST TO CAMP SUNSET

I'll pack my grip [suitcase], *for a farewell trip,*
Kiss Suzy Jane goodbye, at the fountain.
I'm going says I, to the Land of the Sky,
Away Out on the Mountain.

Where the wild sheep grow, and the buffalo low,
And the squirrels are so many, you can't count
    them.
Then I'll make love, to some turtledove,
Away Out on the Mountain.

When the north winds blow, and were gonna'
    have snow,
And the rain and the hail, come bouncing.
I'll wrap myself, in a grizzly bear coat,
Away Out on the Mountain . . .

        Jimmie Rodgers, the early depression-era
                        "singing brakeman"

I t was a memorable day for me when I went through the line at Fort McPherson, Georgia, and found out for certain where I was going. The date was January 8, 1938, and "Fort Mac" was a beehive of activity with hundreds of young men enrolling in the Civilian Conservation Corps.

It seemed to the new recruits, or "rookies" and "new boys" as we were called, that everyplace you looked and everywhere you went there was a line: lines for "chow," clothing, work details, inspections, physicals, and one line that no one liked for "shots," which all recruits received upon entering the CCC. Young men were arriving at the fort for induction into the corps, while others that had been assigned to camps were leaving, making the place look like an anthill.

Fred Arnold, a friend from a community near my hometown, and I had teamed up together at the induction center. Both of us stood among the recruits who were being assigned to camps around the country, receiving traveling orders, and awaiting transportation.

An Army officer was seated at a desk signing up enrollees for CCC camps. When our turn came, he asked if we had a preference of location.

I looked at him and said, "Where is the farthest camp you can send me to from here?"

He looked me over for a long moment, then carefully studied the papers on his desk.

"Vancouver, Washington," he finally replied, "that's as far as I can send you. If you go any farther than that you will be in the Pacific Ocean!"

"Okay, that's where I want to go."

"Me too," said Fred, "that's where I want to go."

The officer then told us that he could put us down for Vancouver because none of the boys who had been through his line had wanted to go that far away from home.

After the enrollment procedures were completed, we were assigned to Army cots in the barracks for our stay at "Fort Mac." We were issued necessities to take with us to our new home in the "Far West," such as shaving kits, towels, barracks bags, and clothes—everything we needed, including Army shoes. After we put on our Army issue clothes, we decided that the military only had two sizes—too big or too little, or, as some of the boys said, "big and bigger."

Even so, I was glad to get them regardless of size or color, as they were good replacements for the worn-out clothes that I had been wearing. By trading with other "rookies," I soon had better fitting clothes, and, with the good food and physical conditioning of the CCC, I quickly gained weight, my muscles filled out, and my clothes fit better than ever.

For ten days after enlisting, I was kept busy with other recruits in a body building program. Barracks duty, exercise, and work details were the order of the day, as we waited for our turn to be sent to CCC camps across the country.

One day, while working on a landscaping detail, I looked up toward the barracks and was startled to see an Army officer riding a beautiful white horse in my direction. He stopped a short distance from where we were working, and watched as we went about our jobs without much enthusiasm, since we wanted to be on a troop train and on our way to the "Far West" instead. I think everyone kept working with their shovels, rakes, and wheelbarrows (commonly called "Georgia Buggies" by the CCC boys) except me. I could only stand and stare at the officer with the stars on his uniform collar sitting on the great white horse.

After he rode off to another area, I asked the crew leader who the impressive officer was, and he informed me that I had been "goldbricking" when I should not have been. The officer I had been staring at was none other than the Commander of the Fourth Corps Area, General George Van Horn Mosley, on a surprise inspection tour.

Later that evening, I paid for my "goldbricking" by having to do extra KP, washing dishes and peeling spuds for the next day's meals. Being on the "black list," however, was of short duration. On the second day after doing extra duty, I was selected, because of my previous experience in the CCC, as an assistant leader on work details from my barracks.

CCC Troop Train

At about 7:00 in the morning, Wednesday, January 19, 1938, we happily boarded a train for the long trip west. It was a CCC "troop train" made up entirely of CCC recruits. The train food, prepared and served Army style, was only fair, but that did not dampen our spirits. Laughing and talking, telling "tall tales," and playing pranks on new found friends kept it from being a dull trip.

Before the trip had ended, many of the boys had earned nicknames that stayed with them as long as they were in the CCC. Each name was attached to a recruit for a reason, though sometimes a poor one, and some names were not very complimentary. One was called "Radio," since he talked all of the time. Another was named "Plow Boy," because of the way he walked. One tall, long legged boy became "High Pockets," and, of course, there was "Shorty," "Slim," "Bean Pole," "Curley," and "Leather Head."

One boy was called "Flag Pole" because, as victim of a prank, he was "assigned" to guard the flag pole his first night at camp. Unaware that he had been tricked, "Flag Pole" diligently stood by the pole till the early hours of the morning, when one of the jokesters finally decided that he had guarded it long enough.

Another was nicknamed "Pee Willy." His real name was Willy. One dark cold night, Willy could not or did not make it to the latrine. He was discovered by the night watchman urinating in the company street. There were other names, too numerous to mention, and some are unprintable, but all were reflective of the fun loving, good natured humor of the CCC lads.

As one youth put it, "I don't care what you call me as long as you show your teeth [smile], and make sure you call me at chow time and payday."

In my first year in the CCC at Camp Hard Labor Creek, I often was called "Lick." After reenlisting for service in the Pacific Northwest, however, I usually was known as "Hill."

Taking photographs along the route and writing letters to friends and relatives helped to pass the time away for many of the enrollees, especially for those who had never been away from home before. These boys felt a little less homesick when they sent a letter or even just a few words jotted down on a picture postcard to family and friends.

The cross-country adventure was a new and never to be forgotten experience for us, most of whom never had been out of the state of Georgia before. It was a wonderful experience for me—an opportunity to travel first class for free and, on top of that, to get paid for it. I thought it was the greatest opportunity of my life. I always had wanted to see what was on "the other side of the Mountain." Now I had the chance to do just that.

We traveled the northern route from Atlanta to Chicago, and on through North Dakota, Montana, and Idaho, to Spokane, and finally to Vancouver, Washington, situated on the north bank of the great Columbia River across from Portland, Oregon. It was wintertime, and the mountains, rolling prairies, and badlands were cold, snow covered, and beautiful.

I never had been in a frigid, icy environment before, or seen a glistening, white landscape like this—a great open space, wild and splendid. In Fargo, North Dakota, and again in Billings, Montana, we got off the train for a few minutes. I am sure the temperature was well below zero in both places. It was a memorable experience for me, something to write home about.

The train carried us through miles of open range, timbered mountains, and great cattle ranches where we could see cowboys on horseback with their livestock. We crossed the Rocky Mountains and the continental divide. These were places that I had studied and read about in school, and had always wanted to see, but I had doubted that I ever would have the opportunity or means to do so. There was abundant wildlife along the way: deer, antelope, jack rabbits with huge ears standing up like sails on a sailboat, coyotes (I thought they were wild dogs until someone told me differently), and even a few buffalo.

A couple of times, we got off the train at stops to exercise and eat our "GI chow" alongside the train. We enjoyed this, even though it was very cold outside. When we stopped at Billings, we were allowed to walk downtown after eating, taking in some fresh, cold Montana air and window-shopping for an hour. Everything was covered with snow, and a cold wind from Canada kept the wind chill factor well below zero.

We were happy to board the train again and enjoy the warmth it offered (along with the candy bars and other small items we had bought). Unlike in the South and East, where numerous cities, towns, villages, and residential districts lined the tracks, we now traveled along mile after mile with no sign of habitation other than wild animals, a few ranch houses, and a road that followed the tracks for miles and then disappeared into the sagebrush, only to reappear again miles farther along the route.

We arrived at Vancouver Barracks in the early morning of January 23, 1938, a day I easily remember—it was my nineteenth birthday. We were eager to get off the train after riding on it for four days and nights, and anxious to see what awaited us. Carrying barracks bags stuffed with clothes and other belongings, we trudged in the rain from the train to the mess hall, where we ate a good breakfast while sitting at a "real table" for the first time in several days.

Sunset Falls in Washington's Cascade Range

After breakfast, the boys assigned to Camp Sunset, F-39, about twenty of us, boarded a canvas covered CCC truck, or "GI bus," for the last leg of the journey. It was cold and rainy, and we were impatient to get to the barracks camp, situated about forty miles northeast of Vancouver in the Cascade Range.

About ten miles from the camp, we were given a good scare by the truck driver, who was accustomed to driving on the narrow, gravel-covered, canyon road. He intentionally sped around hairpin curves and zoomed down narrow stretches where there was only room enough for one vehicle to pass at a time. If two trucks happened to meet, one had to back up to the nearest wide place so the other could get by.

My first impression of the area was not good on the way to the camp, and was even worse when we finally arrived there. It

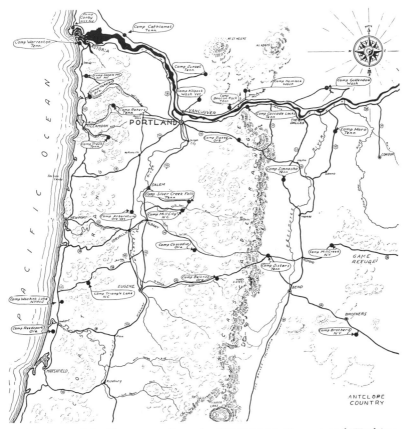

Main camps of the Vancouver Barracks CCC District, Oregon and Washington, 1938. *Official Annual–Vancouver Barracks Civilian Conservation Corps
Ninth Corps Area, 1937*

was chilly, wet, and raining. The locality had been burned over by a great forest fire in 1902 and never recovered. Known as the "Yacolt burn," this great conflagration started September 11-12, 1902, eventually consuming 239,000 acres of timber (or twelve billion board feet) and killing sixteen people. Smoke from the great blaze darkened Seattle, necessitating the use of gas street lights in the early afternoon.

In 1929, 208,000 acres had burned again. Left standing on the hillsides were tottering, fire blackened, snags called "widow-makers" because of the danger they posed to woodsmen when working near them. The place looked lonely and desolate under the dark, rainy skies.

The camp was located ten miles east of Yacolt, Washington, and stood only a short distance, perhaps 200 yards, below Sunset Falls on the East Fork of the Lewis River. It was in what was then known as the Columbia National Forest, but which later, in 1949, was designated as the Gifford Pinchot National Forest in honor of Gifford Pinchot, the first Chief Forester of the U. S. Forest Service.

Camp Sunset was one of the main camps in the Vancouver Barracks Civilian Conservation Corps District. The district embraced over 44,100 square miles of valleys, mountains, forests, lakes, and streams along the southern border of Washington and in western and central Oregon. Each of the district's twenty-eight CCC companies had about 160 to 200 virile young men, all ready and willing to give their best to any task at hand.

By the time I arrived, boys in the Vancouver Barracks CCC District already had strung enough telephone lines to stretch from Vancouver to Chicago, and built enough forest roads and trails to extend from Vancouver to San Francisco and back again. They had constructed ninety-three lookout houses, forty-five lookout towers, and felled hazardous and infested snags on nearly 30,000 acres of burned-over terrain.

Furthermore, the CCC "flame tamers" had spent more than 154,000 man-days fighting and winning battles with the most spectacular enemy of the forest—fire. In fact, fire loss in Washington and Oregon had dropped to the lowest level since the National Forests were established in 1906, thanks to the efforts of the CCC. They also had completed insect control work on 200,000 acres of forest, and built more than 130 miles of fences in livestock country. On the Columbia National Forest, almost all of the trail system had been developed by the CCC.

(A historical footnote—since October 1, 1936, Brigadier General George C. Marshall had commanded the Vancouver Barracks District, overseeing both its military units and the CCC organization in the area. Marshall, of course, soon achieved fame as our nation's wartime Chief of Staff, 1939 to 1945, and as Secretary of State, from 1947 to 1949).

Camp Sunset Founded by Company 945, 1933

Company 945 had built the camp at Sunset Falls in 1933. The advanced detachment of the company was organized May 17, 1933, at Fort Lewis, Washington, and left the next day for Vancouver Barracks, where they spent the night. At the time, Company 945 consisted of two army officers (Captain John G. White and Lieutenant W. E. Read), three enlisted Army men, and twenty-two enrolled members of the Civilian Conservation Corps.

On leaving Vancouver on May 19, these men joined twenty-five enrolled woodsmen (Local Experienced Men, or LEM's) at Sunset Falls. Part of the distance they traveled to get there was on very poor roads.

Before the tents could be pitched in the woods below the falls, a space had to be cleared of logs and snags. The men then lived in this "tent city" while completing the permanent barracks and other facilities. They slept on straw filled mattresses and wooden cots, ate from Army mess kits, and worked seven days a week constructing the camp.

After the camp was completed and occupied by a full complement of men, road building and fire prevention programs were initiated. A year later, in June 1934, the greater part of the company helped fight a destructive flood in Kelso, at the confluence of the Cowlitz and Columbia rivers. A fire lookout also was erected on top of Silver Star Mountain, located five miles "as the crow flies" south of camp, by hauling building materials up a mountain trail by packhorse.

Company 945 remained at Camp Sunset only for a year, or until May 23, 1934, when it began moving to summer quarters at Twin Buttes near Trout Lake in Washington's south-central Cascades. An important project for Company 945 while at the Twin Buttes summer camp was the construction of a road from Twin Buttes to the Lewis River. This joined a road being constructed at the same time down from the north by the Lower Cispus CCC camp. When connected in July 1934, the route provided a link through the mountainous terrain between Trout Lake and Randle.

On October 13, 1934, Company 945 moved to the Rock Creek Camp near the Columbia River, where they spent the winter doing the usual forestry work in the Stevenson vicinity. The enrollees worked and played hard, and had an excellent football team. On July 10, 1935, they moved back to the summer camp at Twin Buttes.

At the end of that summer, an advance crew from Company 945 left Twin Buttes to establish Camp Goldendale in Klickitat County, Washington. The main body followed on October 21. The enrollees were disappointed, however, to find that the new camp was for Soil Conservation Service (SCS) projects in agricultural country, and not forestry work. Many were homesick for the woods, but they soon adjusted to the new location and were happy there.

Camp Goldendale, SCS-8, was rated very high for its achievements. Its educational and recreational activities produced winning teams in basketball, track, baseball, boxing, softball, and wrestling, as well as an unbeaten football team in 1937-1938. Major work accomplished in erosion control included: the construction of 200 permanent rock dams, more than 400 temporary dams, and 20,000 feet of diversion ditches and channels; the development of more than thirty springs on rangeland; and the construction of almost 1,000,000 square yards of bank sloping. Their primary work area was 25,000 acres of cropland and natural pasture in the Swale Creek drainage.

Today, on the slopes of a ditch alongside U. S. Route 97 north of Goldendale, the rock walls built by CCC boys can still be seen.

Camp Sunset in 1938

After Company 945 left Camp Sunset in 1934, other CCC units were stationed at the facility. When I arrived in 1938, it was occupied by Company 5481, which had been organized on October 9, 1936, at Fort Oglethorpe, Georgia.

They had remained in the conditioning camp until October 26, 1936, when they entrained for Somerset, Pennsylvania. They served there nearly a year, until October 7, 1937, when the entire company again boarded a train for the cross-country journey to the Pacific Northwest. After arriving at Vancouver Barracks, they were transported by truck to Camp Sunset. They had been there only a few months when I arrived.

We (the new recruits from "Fort Mac") came into camp near noon and were assigned GI bunks in the barracks. Fred and I were to make our home in "number one barrack," the one farthest from the mess hall (we did not like that), but near to the gravel road running through camp. Our new home also was close to the recreation building and canteen.

We barely had time to throw our barracks bags on assigned bunks when the bugle call to "chow" sounded. We were cold and hungry, and did not waste any time getting to the mess hall where the cooks had prepared our first good hot meal at Camp Sunset. After lunch, we were instructed to check out additional supplies, including bedding, and made up our beds in the prescribed manner. When everything was in its proper place, we were free to look the camp over, and to get acquainted with the personnel.

At 4:00 pm, the work crews arrived back in camp. They had been expecting us, so the fun began immediately. The usual "you'll be sorry" and other catcalls filled the air. Then came the warnings about "hard and dangerous work," "tough foremen," and "rotten food."

After the evening meal, we began to get better acquainted with the "old boys." We had many questions about the camp, the projects we would be working on, the towns nearby, and the recreational possibilities. They asked us about home, if the economy was improving, and if jobs could be found on the "outside." The first night in camp was rough. A few bunks were "tripped," some were "short-sheeted," and at least one had corn flakes scattered in between the sheets.

In the weeks following my arrival, I took every opportunity to discover as much as I could about the camp and the surrounding area. I was impressed with what I found. The camp consisted of four barracks, each housing fifty enrollees, plus a long mess hall and kitchen, a recreation building complete with a canteen or "post exchange," a supply room, a dispensary, the camp commander's office, a woodworking shop, and, across the gravel road from "number one barrack," an educational building. Shower and latrine facilities also were situated conveniently near the barracks.

Located across a tiny spring-fed creek from the main camp stood the project superintendent's office, a toolroom, and the tool repair and saw filing shop, which was one of the busiest places in camp. All the tools used by the enrollees, including picks, shovels, axes, brush hooks, and especially the felling and bucking saws used to cut dead snags on the Yacolt burn, were repaired and sharpened in this building. After a maintenance and safety check, the equipment was stored in the forestry toolroom until needed.

Quarters for Forest Service personnel, including the project superintendent, senior foremen, and special service personnel, likewise were located nearby. A truck shed and vehicle repair shop, with blacksmithing and welding facilities, also stood in this part of the camp.

The East Fork of the Lewis River flowed swiftly over huge rocks, dropping many feet to form beautiful Sunset Falls. The deep pool below the waterfall was a favorite spot for the boys during off duty hours in warm weather. On the horizon, across the river from the camp, stood Silver Star Mountain, with a trail winding up its side to the lookout on top. Situated near the river at the base of Silver Star Mountain was an old abandoned copper mine, as well as a woodcutter's cabin, at a location called "Copper City."

Our water came from a spring on the hillside above the educational building, and flowed through an underground pipeline to camp. A small building later was constructed over the spring while I served at the camp.

A small gasoline powered generator was the sole source of electricity for the camp, necessitating the use of "wood power" for heating and cooking. Lights were turned off in the barracks at 10:00 pm, and the generator was shut down at midnight. The camp remained without electrical power until the generator was started up early the next morning.

Each of the barracks was heated by two woodburning stoves made in the welding shop by enrollees. They were constructed by welding a pair of fifty-five gallon steel drums together in a horizontal position, with a hinged door fitted at one end of the bottom drum. Woodburning ranges were used not only by the camp cooks and for warming the barracks, but also for heating water for showers and other camp use. There was, of course, a plentiful supply of wood in the area.

Our day began with reveille at 5:30, breakfast at 6:00, roll call and sick call at 6:30, and work call at 7:00. Those not confined to camp because of real or faked illness boarded the trucks and were transported to the various work projects in the area. Several maintenance and improvement programs went on simultane-ously: road and trail construction, stringing telephone wires, erecting bridges and fire lookouts, and felling snags, burning slash, and planting trees on the Yacolt burn.

I was assigned to a slash burning crew my first month at Camp Sunset. I wanted to do something different, however, so I took an exam and road test to be a truck driver. A few days later, I was given a license and assigned to a truck, replacing a driver who was discharged to accept other employment. Mr. Celo Anderson, an experienced forester, was my first foreman.

A driver's main responsibility was to transport men and equipment safely to and from work. Each morning, I did a routine safety check on my vehicle before the men boarded with their equipment for the ride out to a project. It also was the duty of the driver to stay near the truck and workers throughout the day, ready to assist if there was an accident or if some other emergency occurred. I was assigned a 1935 1-1/2 ton Chevrolet with a stake bed covered by a heavy canvas tarp.

In addition to transporting men and equipment, the driver also made coffee and set out lunch for the crew at noon. Hot food was served from stainless steel containers. The truck bed served as a "dining room" for the enrollees, and, although crowded, it was a place for the men to eat in inclement weather. Sometimes, sack lunches were prepared by camp cooks for crews unable to get back to the trucks at noon.

In 1938, we constructed a bridge across Copper Creek near where it joins the East Fork of the Lewis River, a short distance upstream from Sunset Falls. Charles Nehr, a Forest Service senior foreman, was the supervisor of the bridge building crew, and other foremen and crews helped when necessary. Still fresh in my memory is an incident at this location that nearly cost me my life.

On the north side of the bridge, there were some huge stumps that had to be cleared from the road. On this particular day, the crew was drilling blasting holes with jackhammers and loading dynamite in preparation for blowing the stumps out. While everyone else was busy, I had nothing to do, so I decided to go for a walk along the river to get away from the noisy jackhammers and air compressors.

I wandered farther and was gone longer than I realized. When I returned, the men and equipment were nowhere in sight. I walked over to a huge stump where they had been working when I left, and stood near it (I believe I actually leaned against it for a moment), while looking around for the men.

Suddenly, I heard someone yell. Rushing toward me came the project foreman, followed closely at his heels by the blasting crew. He ran up to me and gave me the worst "eyeball to eyeball" chewing out that I ever received in my three years in the CCC.

While I was gone, they had completed the drilling, loaded the boreholes with dynamite, put the electric blasting caps in place, and set the wiring to fire the charge off. If it had gone off as planned, as they were trying to do as I unknowingly stood next to the charges, I would have been blasted to bits along with the stump! Luckily, the wiring to the blasting machine had not been properly connected, causing a malfunction.

Safety was the number one priority in the CCC, and all the proper procedures had been carefully followed by the foreman in charge. All personnel had been ordered out of the blasting zone, road blocks were set up to prevent anyone from entering the area, and the location of all workers was accounted for. All, that is, except me, the truck driver, whom they assumed was in his truck and parked a safe distance away. The last and final warning had been shouted—"Fire in the hole!"—before the downward thrust of the rack bar into the blasting machine. The incident could have been entirely avoided, of course, if I had remained "on the job," instead of wandering along the riverbank daydreaming.

About two weeks later, I was ordered to haul a load of explosives from Sunset Falls to Camp Hemlock, located near Carson, Washington, a distance of about thirty miles. Again, all safety precautions were observed. A route was carefully planned out following forest roads over the mountains. No other cargo was allowed in the vehicle with the dynamite, and especially no passengers! The truck was fitted with two large "EXPLOSIVES" signs, front and rear. For additional safety, two vehicles were assigned to accompany me to Carson, one ahead and one in back.

I was cautioned to drive with extreme care on the rough roads just as if I were hauling eggs. If a lightning storm occurred along the way, I was told to pull off the road, park the truck, and "run like hell" away from the vehicle, and to stay away from it until the storm passed. Still shaky from my close call at the bridge construction site, I hauled my first load of dynamite with much caution and respect. It was with great relief that I arrived at my destination without incident.

While residing in a barracks with about fifty boys, we rubbed shoulders with all types of personalities, from the weakest to the strongest. As I mentioned earlier, we had to learn how to cope with the different kinds of situations that naturally arise in group living. This skill has proven to be of inestimable value to us ever since.

Our activities during off duty hours in the barracks were varied. In the early evening, as a few boys "hit the sack" early to sleep or read, others wrote letters or studied, while, at the same time, a card game might be going on atop a bunk or footlocker. There usually was some "horse play," and someone sewing on a button or mending a pair of pants. We also enjoyed singing.

There always was a musical instrument available, usually a guitar, and we would gather around and sing songs from memory or from a CCC song book containing "golden oldies" and parodies. "Leather Head" Whitfield, a boy from the mountains of North Carolina, was well-known for his homespun jokes and descriptive language. He often came forth with lyrics of unknown origin, singing them with great gusto.

One of his favorites was, "The old apple tree—it reminds me of my Pappy, he was handsome, young, and happy, when he planted the old apple tree."

"Rookies," not used to barracks life, quickly learned to ignore loud noise and "horsing around." Later in the evening, as the boys quieted down, someone would turn on a radio to listen to the popular "Big Bands" of the era. Although the enrollee who owned the radio could have listened to anything he wanted, he graciously let others take turns at tuning in programs throughout the evening. Consequently, we heard "Swing and Sway with Sammy Kay" or the Benny Goodman Band, when he, perhaps, rather would have listened to "Wayne King the Waltz King" or "The Sweetest Music This Side of Heaven" orchestra of Guy Lombardo. I enjoyed all of the great bands, but among my favorites were Tommy Dorsey, Artie Shaw, and Fred Waring.

Once a year, the enrollees held an open house, banquet, and dance for local residents in the area. It was the big event of the year—windows were washed, trucks and equipment were lined up in the proper places, the barracks were scrubbed, and the recreation building was decorated. The boys were all primed for the occasion, with fresh haircuts and wearing well polished GI boots and their best clothes.

Our cooks prided themselves on their skill, and they made a special effort to prepare a fine banquet. The salads and desserts were excellently done, roasts and hams were cooked to perfection, and the punch was a superb concoction, specifically prepared for the event.

Before dinner, the guests were conducted on a full circuit of the camp, including the barracks, forestry headquarters, and the educational facilities. The auto repair shop and truck shed, where the washed and polished vehicles were lined up, also was included in the tour.

After a fine dinner served in the mess hall, which had been decorated by the cooks and KP's, the boys and their guests enjoyed an evening of dancing to the music of a local band that donated their time for the occasion. One of my close buddies, nicknamed "Nanners," decided to help out the musicians with his own rendition of a song. As the couples danced to "Sugar Foot Rag," he made his way through the crowd to the raised orchestra platform, proudly brought his six-foot-plus frame to attention, and began singing "Flat Foot Floogie with the Flowery Drawers." But, his spontaneous lyrics and tune differed from the song the band was playing. We did not let "Nanners" forget that performance for a long time.

There was little reason for anyone to be bored and lonely, or without something useful to do to occupy their time. We kept a full schedule, with our work, evening classes, and recreational programs. The number of boys interested in basketball was large enough to form the "Rebels," a team that played (and lost) many games while competing with other CCC camps and local "civilian" teams. There was considerable interest in wrestling and boxing, but wrestling was curtailed after one of the boys badly injured his back in a match in the recreation hall (that enrollee, now a retired senior citizen, still suffers from the injury).

The boxers continued to train in camp and competed with amateurs at "smokers" in nearby towns, which were well attended by enrollees and local citizens. Our CCC "champ" was a lightweight boxer answering to the nickname "Speedy," who won several local tournaments.

CCC Sponsored Educational Opportunities

While in the 3C's, I took a number of educational courses. I completed high school, as well as correspondence courses in forestry, and in fire presuppression from the California State Department of Education, and also first aid and automobile mechanic classes taught at camp. There were other courses that I wanted to sign up for, such as photography, welding, and woodworking, but a forty-hour work week and my other educational commitments did not leave enough time for more study.

Education was not a priority when the Civilian Conservation Corps was originally established in April 1933. Robert Fechner, the first national CCC director (1933-1939), had believed that enrollees must work a full forty-hour week, and that they had to do an honest day's work every day. He felt that the CCC should not provide educational programs—that the camps were places to learn how to work, to live, and to get ahead with practical laboring experience. By late 1933, however, overwhelming pressure from President Roosevelt, government agencies, educators, and the public forced Fechner (and the U. S. Army) to allow for the adoption of a full-fledged educational system in the CCC camps.

In November 1933, FDR put his stamp of approval on developing educational programs in the CCC. The average enrollee was nineteen years of age and had completed 8-1/2 years of schooling. Five percent of the enlistees were classified as totally illiterate. By 1937, 50,000 illiterates were taught to read and write, and were graduated from a grade school curriculum set up by the CCC. Another 400,000 had received high school instruction, and, altogether, 40,000 college courses had been taken by enrollees.

The success of the CCC study program was attested to by the fact that educational administrators in forty-seven states and the District of Columbia issued regulations accrediting classes taught in the camps. The training and educational system was intensified and expanded from 1934 until the CCC was disbanded in 1942.

The educational programs at the camps in which I served were excellent. We were encouraged to take as many classes as we had the time and energy for after an eight-hour workday, and there were numerous subjects to choose from. The instruction at camp and the correspondence courses were free.

The first class I completed was practical law, taught at Camp Hard Labor Creek during my first year in the 3C's. It was a long and difficult course, requiring much study on my part. Only a few boys were interested in it, so it was a small class. The teacher was a conscientious and dedicated professional, otherwise I would not have finished the course. With patience, persuasion, and understanding, he helped me complete the unit of study.

Jessie Davis was a motherly, middle-aged lady who taught art in her small cottage at Yacolt, Washington. She encouraged any enrollee interested in art to attend her classes for free. "Miss Jessie," as she was fondly called by the boys, also was a writer of poems and stories.

She wrote a manuscript titled *Legend of the Bridge of the Gods*, which explained the Indian myth about the role of Mt. Adams in forming the "Bridge of the Gods" on the Columbia River. Because it was my favorite story, she gave me the typed manuscript. I treasured it for years, until it was lost along with some other keepsakes while I was serving in the U. S. Army during World War II.

She was not only a fine art teacher and storyteller, but also a special friend of the 3C's boys. She will always be remembered for her kindness and compassion. We enjoyed the homey atmosphere, and the pie, cookies, and hot coffee she prepared for us. Unfortunately, I attended only a few classes. I had to quit because I already was too busy with my other studies and work.

Memoirs of Victor Snyder, Camp Sunset, 1933-1934

Victor Snyder, from Kelso, Washington, joined the 3C's on June 3, 1933, and arrived at Camp Sunset within a few days of its establishment. He aptly describes what an enrollee's life was like in the earliest days of the CCC. Snyder begins his account with his induction at Vancouver Barracks:

"On arriving at Vancouver, we were given physical examinations and shots. On Sunday, June 4, 1933, the day before we were sent out, some of the boys went into town, while most of us remained at the fort. They 'rolled us out' of bed early Monday morning, loaded us in old Army trucks of 1918 vintage (which was the best equipment they had), and we headed out. No one knew where we were going, except the driver, until we entered the big Yacolt burn, a fire ravaged area measuring about twenty by forty miles.

"When we arrived at Sunset Falls, it was raining, and LEM's from Vancouver, Battle Ground, and Amboy and some recruits already were there, building the camp. They had cleared some ground and showed us a place where we could put our tents. No one knew how to pitch a sixteen-by-sixteen feet pyramid tent, I can assure you, especially in the rain. But we finally got some tents up, and the next morning started clearing ground for facilities to house 200 enrollees. The rest of the complement of men were coming in from Fort Lewis in a few weeks.

"We slept on wooden bunks, which stood two high, and were given straw ticks for mattresses. We used straw from hay bales to fill the mattress covers. Having no pillows, we used our coats and what have you to lay our heads on, and each of us was issued two blankets. The tents were adequately warmed by small airtight heaters.

"There was some kind of a cook tent set up where 'chow' was prepared. All the time I was in the CCC, we used Army mess kits. We had no ceramic dishes, plates, or other fancy tableware; we just had mess kits and washed them in a tub of water as we left the eating area.

"During the first month, there were no days off, or really any time off at all. We worked seven days a week trying to get the buildings up, and, as I remember, we did pretty well. We finished the cookhouse, the barracks were almost completed, and it was not long before the officers' quarters would be done also. When the other recruits arrived, of course, the structures just had an outside sheathing; there was no finish on the inside of any kind.

"After the camp was built and the other boys arrived, we started clearing 100-yard wide firebreaks on the ridges to halt forest fires should they break out. After cutting up snags and downed timber, the boys used 'peavies' to roll the logs into piles for burning. I believe we had about thirty-five teams of 'fallers' and 'buckers' out at a time working on the firebreaks.

"Also, if I remember correctly, we built approximately seventy miles of road and surfaced most of that with gravel from a rockcrusher operated by CCC boys. The roads were not superhighways by any means, but they were passable.

"Most of the enrollees constructed roads or cut firebreaks, but we also erected the lookout station on top of Silver Star Mountain, located several miles south of camp. The lumber and everything else used to build it was hauled by packhorse up a steep trail to the summit.

"There was an old shack and a couple of mine shafts at the foot of Silver Star Mountain, and one of the boys said that he had talked to a man there once, but I do not think anyone stayed there full time while I was at Camp Sunset. I bought a book on ghost towns in Washington some years ago, which identified that spot as 'Copper City.' Well, I do not know who would ever find it now. I was up there several years ago and could not locate it.

"I also visited the site of the old CCC camp. All that is there now is a little sign on a tree identifying Camp Sunset and some picnic tables. So much brush has grown up that I did not even attempt to go down to the river. Logging operations were going on, cutting down trees we planted up there a half-century ago. I have forgotten how many hundreds of thousands of trees we planted, but it was a lot. We did much good; we did more than pay our way at Camp Sunset.

"There was no camp newspaper, but one time we did get about ten or fifteen books from the library in Vancouver. As I remember, that was all the 'library' we had. In this period, there were no teachers assigned to the camp, nor did anyone come in to give instruction.

"We eventually had a doctor stationed with Company 945, who also served at Speelyai and another camp on the Lewis River. One of the CCC boys was his assistant, and drove him back and forth to the other camps. They were gone a couple of days a week.

"I was in charge of the toolhouse at the camp. I replaced axe, sledgehammer, and small tool handles, constructed spring-boards, and kept track of tools and equipment. I even made shoe and boot grease from a recipe provided by the Army or the Forest Service. If I remember correctly, it contained coal tar, kerosene, and beeswax. I mixed the ingredients by hand, and it seemed to be good grease because the boys never complained about water leaking into their boots.

"In those early days of the CCC, we did not have baseball or basketball teams or any form of organized recreation; we were sent there to work, and work we did. Other companies in our district always received higher ratings from the Army for neatness; one camp in particular had well kept, whitewashed buildings and was landscaped with decorative rows of painted rocks. We ended up at the bottom of the list for appearance, but, when it came to work accomplished, our company was tops. We knew we were there to work and not to make the camp look beautiful. We figured no one wanted to come up there to look us over anyway.

"The first officers were Captain John G. White, of the regular Army, and Lieutenant Read, a reservist, who was second in command. Sergeant Anderson ran the mess hall, and Corporal Coker was in charge of supplies. A man from Battle Ground operated the canteen and filled in as company clerk.

"They issued us old 'choker' Army pants of World War I vintage, and overcoats that flared out at the bottom and were very heavy. [Old fashioned Army trowsers sometimes were called "choker" or "pistol legged" pants by enrollees, because the legs were so tight. CCC boys sometimes spliced the lower pant legs and cuffs, sewing in pieces of Army blankets to make them wider—Ed Hill.] We were given good shoes and socks, however, and received a blue fatigue hat, in contrast to our 'OD' [olive drab] Army clothes. All in all, we were anything but stylish.

"In about mid May 1934, Company 945 was transferred to a summer camp at Twin Buttes near Big Mosquito Lake. We were just west of the Cascade divide and about forty miles north of White Salmon, Washington. When they named Big Mosquito Lake, they were correct. We set up sixteen-by-sixteen feet pyramid tents with mosquito nets over the bunks to ward off swarms of the pesky insects.

"It was a small camp with only about fifty boys, whose main duty was road building. A road that we worked on went north toward the Lewis River to meet another road being built out of Randle by a CCC camp stationed on the Cispus River. Whichever crew reached the river first was to get the honor of building the bridge across the stream. When I left on July 7, 1934, the crews were close enough that we could hear blasting being done by the Randle boys. The crews met at the river about the middle of July.

"One time, while I was home on leave in Kelso, rising floodwater had broken through the dikes close to the mouth of the Cowlitz River, and flowed into the south section of town, backing up into the business district. I helped my mother move out of our house, and put a few sandbags in the dike before returning to camp as my weekend leave expired.

"When I arrived back at camp, 100 men were ready to pull out and go down to Kelso to help patrol the town, man the dikes, and do other flood control work. I received permission to join them. We were transported in new 1933 Chevrolet trucks, with air in the tires instead of hard rubber wheels like on the old 1918 Army trucks.

"We were transported to Kelso, and stationed in the Cowlitz School in west Kelso near the flooded area, so people would not loot and ransack houses and businesses. I was just a little over a block from where I lived, but one would have had to have been a good swimmer to get there. Our house sat on a little knoll. Although water was all around, none got in the home. We were fortunate. Many of our neighbors were completely washed out. We were there a week or ten days before returning to camp and our regular duties.

"The only memorabilia I now have from my days in the 3C's is a stainless steel mirror that was issued for shaving, and, I think, an old CCC ring that cost maybe fifty cents and is badly tarnished. There were no shoulder patches or insignias on our uniforms in those early days of the CCC, as there were later."

A. G. StJohn at Camp Sunset, 1937-1940

A. G. StJohn served at the Sunset Falls camp from the autumn of 1937 until the company disbanded on August 17, 1940. He was assigned to Camp Sunset a few months before my arrival. StJohn's reminiscences begin with his first impressions of the locality:

"We reached the Sunset Falls CCC camp on October 11, 1937, and a notation in my diary reads, 'Falls very beautiful, Camp F-39 not so good.' It was located in an area of the old Columbia National Forest that had been badly burned over. Standing all around was a dead forest of tall, bare snags that once had been living trees—one of the most desolate places many of us had ever seen. It was cold and raining; in fact, it always seemed to be raining, which took some effort to get used to.

"I was assigned to the project superintendent's office as a clerk, and shortly was promoted to leader, and things began to look good again. We learned later that Camp Sunset was a 'winter' camp. In June, the company would be moved to a 'summer' location deep in the Cascades (Camp Skamania in the Trout Lake vicinity), where we would live in tents until October, before striking camp and returning to Sunset Falls.

"Life in the winter at Sunset Falls was relatively relaxed and routine, and, once we got used to the weather, quite enjoyable. We were welcomed in the local communities, and eagerly looked forward to the dances put on by the grange halls. I made many friendships during the three years there, many of which I cherish to this day. And, of course, there were several marriages between our boys and the local girls.

"In contrast to winter quarters, the summer camp routine was frantic. We usually were on alert for fire fighting duty. Isolated deep in the forest, we were kept 'at the ready' even on weekends. Recreational trips, which were commonplace while in winter camp, were few and far between during the summer.

"On the rare occasion when summer rains lessened the fire danger, we would, when granted a weekend pass, head for White Salmon, Vancouver, or Portland. I spent many enjoyable weekends with Mr. Edmond C. Hanson, one of our foremen, at his home in Portland. We usually ended up at the Jantzen Beach ballroom where big name bands, such as Benny Goodman's, played."

"Junior enrollee" Ed Hill, seventeen years of age, at Camp Hard Labor Creek, SP-11, near Rutledge, Georgia, circa 1936. *Edwin G. Hill*

Camp Sunset, F-39, located east of Yacolt in Washington's southern Cascade Range. The great Yacolt burn of 1902 had destroyed the forests in this locality. *Edwin G. Hill*

Jack Martin, from Atlanta, Georgia, at Sunset Falls on the East Fork of the Lewis River. *Edwin G. Hill*

Times were hard in Georgia, but people maintained their dignity. My sister, Henriella Hill Poole, with her sons, Grover (left) and William (right), circa early 1940s. *Edwin G. Hill*

Spike camp on Silver Star Mountain; cutting firebreaks through the dead snags. *Gifford Pinchot National Forest*

"Big Foot" Johnson (right) and Ed Hill, Camp Sunset, 1939. *Edwin G. Hill*

Twin Buttes Lookout, with Mt. St. Helens in the distance. *Clayton Strandberg*

Camp Skamania at Smokey Creek in the shadow of Mt. Adams; summer quarters for boys from Camp Sunset. *Gifford Pinchot National Forest*

Indians in the Twin Buttes/Indian Heaven locality, mid 1930s. *Gifford Pinchot National Forest*

Picking "olallies" (huckleberries). *Gifford Pinchot National Forest*

Huckleberries drying in the sun. *Gifford Pinchot National Forest*

Indian encampment, with Mt. Adams to the east. *Gifford Pinchot National Forest*

"My 'two' friends and I"; H. C. Martin (left) and Ed Hill at Camp Skamania on Smokey Creek, 1939. *Edwin G. Hill*

Jessie Davis of Yacolt, Washington; "Miss Jessie" taught art to the Camp Sunset enrollees. *Edwin G. Hill*

"Baby," mascot at the Cougar side camp. *Edwin G. Hill*

Velma Barger and Ed Hill, wedding day, September 22, 1939. *Edwin G. Hill*

On the fire line in a western forest. *Manuscripts, Archives, and Special Collections, Washington State University Library, Pullman*

Chapter Five

CAMP SKAMANIA AND MT. ADAMS

S – is for the spuds we get for breakfast.
H – is for the home we seldom see.
O – is for the onions that they feed us.
V – is for this verse composed by me.
E – is for the end of my enlistment.
L – is for the last they'll see of me.
Put them all together they spell SHOVEL
The emblem of the CCC.

Fort Lewis CCC songbook, 1934

T he announcement that the entire company would move from Sunset Falls to Camp Skamania for the summer fire season caused much excitement. We began our preparations, and, by early summer, had transported all of the equipment and 200 men to the summer camp, located 145 miles away. The move was completed in good time, without any major problems or unusual incidents, by a fleet of CCC trucks operated by the enrollees.

Camp Skamania was located twelve miles west of Trout Lake, Washington, next to a small mountain stream called Smoky (now Smokey) Creek. The site offered a spectacular view of beautiful Mt. Adams standing about a dozen miles to the northeast; its 12,325 feet peak remained ice covered year around.

Wild country surrounded us in every direction, but the extensive tract to the west was especially primitive. In this roadless area were volcanic craters, alpine meadows, old growth forests, more than 150 lakes, and an old historic race track where Indians ran horses during summer sojourns in the mountains in the last century. Today, this locality, with its breath-taking scenery, is designated as the Indian Heaven Wilderness, and is traversed by sixty miles of hiking trails. The last horses were run on the circular, mountain-meadow race track in 1928, but, afterwards, Indians still returned to nearby localities to pick vast quantities of huckleberries (more about this later).

There were only four permanent structures at Camp Skamania: a mess hall, a shower and latrine facility, a garage, and a forestry building, which included the company commander's office. Enrollees were housed in Army pyramid tents lined up on each side of a company street. Each tent was equipped with six Army bunks, a small woodburning stove for heat, and mosquito nets. The camp's gasoline-powered generator produced only enough electricity for lights in our "tent city."

A detachment of about forty men, or one-fourth of the company, including a foreman, cook, truck drivers, and other camp staff, were sent to a side camp at Twin Buttes, located about ten miles northwest of Smokey Creek. They were available for emergency fire duty while working on projects in that area, and remained there until the fire season ended in the fall.

Numerous projects had been planned for us as soon as we were situated in our "summer homes." We were kept very busy during the two summers (in 1938 and 1939) that I was stationed at Smokey Creek: we were trained to fight forest fires; we built and maintained firebreaks, roads, and trails; we patrolled the roads when fire danger was extremely high; and we improved and maintained campgrounds from Peterson Prairie to Big

Mosquito Lake. Not least among the varied tasks carried out by Company 5481 was the operation of a rockcrusher located near camp. It supplied all of the gravel used on the roads in that section of the National Forest.

One notable project was the construction of the Peterson Prairie visitors' center, which served to inform the public about the many campgrounds and extensive huckleberry fields in this part of the Cascade Range. It was a fine peeled log structure, and remains in good condition today. Campgrounds, complete with tables, stone fireplaces, and water spigots, all built by the CCC boys, also remain in use today, though sometimes needing repairs.

The largest and most popular campground was at Cultus Creek, where a country store was operated to serve campers. At the height of the summer season, all of the campgrounds were filled to capacity with campers from as far away as Seattle, Portland, and the Yakima Valley. Visitors set up tents for a weekend, for a week or two, or even for all summer. Many came to pick and sell wild huckleberries to buyers, who resold them in the cities.

The nation, of course, still was in the grasp of the Great Depression, though the economy was not quite as bad off as it had been in the early to mid 1930s. The opportunity to camp-out, and earn money at the same time, was appreciated by visitors to the National Forest.

In addition to enjoying the scenery and fresh air, campers enjoyed the camaraderie among the visitors to the campgrounds. Their evenings were filled with storytelling, laughter, and merry-making. For some, friendships were made that lasted a lifetime, and romances among the youths were common.

Enrollees participated in these campground activities as much as time and duty permitted, visiting both the young and not-so-young, which reminded the boys of the "old folks" at home. Many long evenings were enjoyed around bonfires at the Cultus Creek and Little Goose campgrounds (fire danger permitting, of course), singing or dancing to the accompaniment of a guitar or violin, usually played by CCC boys.

When the danger of forest fires breaking out was at its greatest, usually in the dry weeks of late summer, enrollees were confined to camp, where they remained on alert. The mental strain from the prospect of fighting fires could cause the enrollees to be extremely tense, but the boys quickly snapped out of it when the fire danger passed, or they actually were sent out on the fire line. Within minutes, after an alarm was given, drivers on standby duty went into action, pulling their trucks off the "ready line." The enrollees jumped into the trucks with their equipment and supplies, and were off.

They were transported as close to a fire as possible, and then proceeded on foot the remaining distance, sometimes packing their fire fighting equipment several miles. Many a forest fire was quickly brought under control, contained, and extinguished, due to the quick response of the CCC "tree troopers." Some fires were started by lightning, others by the campfires of careless campers or huckleberry pickers, and some by irresponsible smokers throwing lit cigarettes out along trails or roadways.

Along with my other truck driving duties, I patrolled the forest roads for many hours, night and day, on the alert for fires. I kept an especially close watch around campgrounds and along roadways, where fire danger was greatest. I enjoyed fire patrol duty immensely, since it was more exciting than our regular routine.

It provided me with an opportunity to assist with CCC chores in the campgrounds, such as unloading the heavy picnic tables built by enrollees, and to get acquainted with campers. I kept a sufficient supply of freshly brewed coffee, sugar, and canned milk in my truck not only for the workers, but also for forest visitors.

Indian Encampments

Wild huckleberries grow abundantly in vast patches in the meadows and mountains of the Cascade Range. Deep snow buries the huckleberry bushes during the long winter months, but, following the spring melt, they come alive, producing great amounts of tasty, juicy, red-blue berries.

From time immemorial, Indians had journeyed great distances to harvest and dry huckleberries for winter food. Many traditional customs and ceremonies had developed around the picking, preserving, and consumption of the berries—most notably, an annual huckleberry feast.

In the late 1930s (and today), Indians had preferential rights in some localities near Mt. Adams. Traditionally-used berry fields were set aside for their exclusive use, according to the terms of the Walla Walla Treaty, which dates back to 1855 and remains in effect today. In the Surprise Lakes and Cold Spring area, there are warning signs posted, alerting visitors to the fact that the huckleberry patches on the east side of the Forest Service road are reserved exclusively for Indians.

The Meadow Creek, Surprise Lakes, and Cold Spring campgrounds used by the Indians are located in a beautiful subalpine setting with an impressive view of white capped Mt. Adams (named by the Indians "Phato," meaning "Sacred Mountain"). Each year, I saw Indians—men, women, the young and old—come to the high country on ponies, in horse drawn wagons, as well as by truck and automobile. They included Indians from the Warm Springs reservation in Oregon, the Klickitat whose ancestral lands originally were directly to the south in the Goldendale area, and the Yakima from the Yakima reservation to the east.

It was an unforgettable sight, encountering a caravan of wagons loaded down with camping equipment and supplies en route to the berry fields, with men and women walking alongside or riding on horseback and in buggies. Upon their arrival, a camping site was selected near the choicest huckleberry patches. They quickly unloaded and skillfully set up poles for tepees. Within a short time, the supplies and equipment were stored away, a campfire was started, and all was made ready for beginning the berry harvest.

From the road, Indians could be seen picking berries, called by them "olallies," while others tended the camps, where children played and babies slept. After the pickers filled their handwoven baskets, they covered them with a pad of leaves to preserve the berries. The leaves kept the berries cool and fresh for several days, until enough could be gathered to be processed for later use.

Observing the Indians picking berries, their picturesque camps, and their carefree lifestyle was one of my most memorable experiences during the two years that I served in the CCC in the shadow of Mt. Adams.

Baptism of Fire, 1938

Of the enemies of the forest—known as the "Three horsemen: fire, insects, and disease"—fire is, of course, the most spectacular. It destroys timber, watersheds, wildlife habitat, and recreational and scenic sites. Annually, thousands of acres of valuable forest are burned at a cost of many thousands of dollars to the taxpayer and the lumber industry. Fire fighters frequently are injured, and occasionally killed. Years of additional labor and expenditures are required for reforestation, habitat rehabilitation, and wildlife replenishment.

I had my "baptism of fire" while stationed at Camp Skamania in the summer of 1938. A blaze started to the north in the Randle/Packwood area, requiring much time and effort to control. The fire danger was extremely high in the forest at the time, and all the available men and equipment were desperately needed to extinguish "spot fires" throughout the area.

While on patrol duty driving along the road from Peterson Prairie to Cultus Creek, a distance of about nine miles, I received an emergency call. I was ordered to return to camp, and prepare to transport a fire fighting detail to Camp Lower Cispus, which served as fire fighting headquarters in the Randle/Packwood locality.

Within a short period of time—only moments from receiving the order—my truck was back at Camp Skamania, and loaded with men and equipment. We set out on the road recently completed through the timbered, mountainous country between

Twin Buttes and Randle. It was early evening and getting dark. The route was little more than a trail, barely wide enough for the truck to pass through in places.

As I drove the narrow, winding road along the canyons and cliffs, I came upon a sharp horseshoe bend. Not seeing the curve in time to negotiate it, I instead braked to a shuddering halt to prevent plunging off the roadway. I had to back the truck up a few yards, then proceeded on cautiously, with all due respect for the deep canyon alongside the road.

When we arrived, the Camp Lower Cispus men already were hard at work trying to contain the fire, and they were glad to see us. We had to remain on the fire line until the blaze either was brought under control or we were relieved by another crew of "flame tamers." This was my first "big one," and I was excited, being on the fire line fighting a "real live one" alongside enrollees from two camps.

The Cispus fire was the largest and most destructive of the 1938 fire season in that area. It destroyed hundreds of acres of prime timber, and required the combined efforts of the Skamania and Lower Cispus camps and all available local men to battle. We slept any place made available to us—the CCC camp recreational building, the Randle school gym, or on the ground in sleeping bags supplied by the Forest Service. Food was prepared at the CCC camp kitchen by cooks from both camps.

I was on the front line for about a week, before being sent back to do fire patrol duty at Smokey Creek. It had been hard work, but it was a great adventure for the 3C's boys to participate in fighting the "big one" of the season. We were glad, of course, when we returned to camp to sleep in a clean bed with springs.

I must point out one fact, though. My duties were comparatively easy compared to those of some others, especially the boys who packed gasoline-powered water pumps and hundreds of feet of hose into hot spots, or the enrollees who used crosscut saws and hand tools to construct firebreaks or do other fire suppression work.

Mountain Climber Rescued

Also during the summer of 1938, an attempt was made to clear terrain for a ski run on the south side of Mt. Adams near the Trout Lake/Mt. Adams road. A senior foreman, a truck driver, and a small crew of men from Smokey Creek set up a side camp there. Included in this group was Fred Arnold, who had joined the CCC's with me at Fort McPherson, Georgia.

When not fighting fire, they worked at clearing the slopes for the ski run; but the project later was abandoned. Fred related to me an account about his participation in the rescue of a mountain climber on Mt. Adams.

Against the advice of the Forest Service, three men were climbing the peak from the Trout Lake side in very icy conditions. One of them slipped off a ledge, falling into an extremely slick, bowl-like cavity. He slid down the ice so fast that he did not come to a stop at the bottom, but slid partway up the other side, and then back down again, finally coming to a stop at the bottom of the hole, badly bruised and with a broken leg.

While one of the climbers stayed with the injured man, the other went to the CCC camp at timberline seeking help. Quickly, a crew left the camp in a truck driven by Fred Arnold, who transported them as near as possible to the mountain. The CCC boys were accompanied by an Army rescue team.

Climbing to the scene of the accident, they chipped steps in the ice down to the injured man, and let down a sled-like contraption. A member of the rescue team tied the climber on it, and the men on top pulled the injured man up.

Safety Officer Forced Off the Road

Driving a truck in the CCC was an interesting and rewarding experience, and a job that I enjoyed very much. The list of duties for a truck driver went on and on—I took enrollees to town during off duty hours, drove on fire patrol, hauled equipment and supplies, and transported men to jobs. All the time, I had to maintain and service my vehicle.

There was one incident during the summer of 1938, however, that marred my safety record. I was driving a truck heavily loaded with gravel down a long steep grade between Smokey Creek and Peterson Prairie.

The narrow road had several sharp curves, and I came onto one too fast, taking the inside—the wrong side—to keep from tipping over. Exactly at that moment, another vehicle came right at me around the curve. We would have collided head on if the other driver had not responded instantly. He turned his steering wheel sharply, driving off the road into the forest, narrowly missing trees, but preventing a head-on crash.

I did not stop, but only slowed down enough for a quick look to see if the driver was okay, then proceeded on to my destination. When I returned to camp at the end of the workday, the shop foreman, Ed Hanson, was waiting for me "with blood in his eye." He told me that the vehicle I had almost collided with was driven by none other than a high ranking CCC safety officer from the Northwest regional forest office in Portland. He was on his way to our camp to inspect facilities and equipment.

Hanson then ushered me into the office of Mr. Alex McKay, the project superintendent, who was waiting for me. McKay told me in no uncertain language that of all the "blankety-blank" vehicles to force off the road into the woods, it had to be none other than the safety inspector's!

He then informed me very positively: "You are grounded and now you will work on a crew with a muckstick [pick or shovel] until I decide to let you drive again."

The next morning, you can believe that I was not very happy about the situation as I went to work with a trail building crew. McKay relented after about a week, however, due to the extra demands of fire season, combined with all of our other work projects. I returned to driving a truck. McKay was certain that I had learned a lesson.

I continued driving a vehicle for the remaining time I served in the 3C's. You can be sure that I was a very careful driver after that incident. During the following year, I assisted with driver education classes after work hours, and, on Saturdays, gave lessons to enrollees selected from a roster of applicants.

Off Duty Hours

Some of the most enjoyable experiences in the 3C's were our trips into town on weekends. While stationed at Smokey Creek, we went to White Salmon, or to Bingen, about a mile farther "down the hill" from White Salmon, on the Columbia River.

The roller skating rink in White Salmon was popular with many of the boys. Others preferred the movies, or eating, drinking, and dancing, at times getting unruly. Most of us were under the legal drinking age of twenty-one, but we often acquired alcohol anyway.

On one occasion, several of us went into a restaurant in Bingen to "slurp a few suds" (beers) and eat. When the waitress came to take our orders, a forestry foreman, well-known for his colorful language, ordered a steak.

As the waitress asked him how he wanted it cooked, he said, "Just knock the horns off the 'S.O.B.' and drive him in."

En route to White Salmon, we passed through a small village called BZ Corner, located at a remote crossroads far from any sizeable town. BZ Corner consisted of a few houses, occupied by loggers and several other residents, as well as a large dance hall that was a popular local gathering place. Almost every time I passed through there with a load of enrollees going to town, a few boys would stop off, and I would pick them up later when returning to camp.

One time, I stopped by about midnight to pick up the boys. They all boarded the truck except "Nub," who was too inebriated and fell underneath the truck bed. At every attempt to stand upright, his head struck the underside of the vehicle. Too drunk to understand where he was, he thought someone was beating him on the head.

He said after each attempt to get up, "Don't hit me again."

After letting him try to stand up a few times, we picked him up and laid him on the floor of the truck for the rough ride back to camp. The jolting over the forest road sobered him enough so that he managed to climb off the truck at camp without any assistance. Long afterwards, his friends continued to laugh about the incident, much to his embarrassment. Usually, our off duty excursions were orderly, and seldom were there any difficulties between the CCC boys and the "natives."

The enrollees, while stationed in winter quarters at Camp Sunset, were driven to Vancouver to attend movies, dances, and sporting events, or just to see the sights. From Vancouver, some boys walked on the interstate bridge across the Columbia River to Jantzen Beach on the Oregon shore, where a giant roller coaster was a main attraction in an amusement park. Several times, I hitchhiked with A. G. StJohn, Buck Jordon, and Fred Arnold to Portland to attend dances at McElroy's Spanish Ballroom, one of our favorite places for dancing and entertainment.

There were other pleasant events that I recollect from my time at Camp Skamania. July 24, 1939, in particular, is a date well remembered. I was working on a road improvement project several miles from camp, transporting the crew and equipment to the work site. At the end of the workday, the men quickly boarded the truck, eager to get back to camp for showers, food, and some free time. On the way to the CCC camp, the road passed by three campgrounds in the cool, picturesque forest, all filled to capacity with campers.

As I drove slowly past the Smokey Creek Campground, my eyes focused on a beautiful, auburn haired young woman, slim and rather tall, with all parts in excellent proportion. She was standing in front of a tent near an open campfire, and I almost stopped the truck. I found out later that her whole family, including a cousin, a redhead, were in the camp, but I only saw her.

I said to the crew leader riding with me, "Did you see that girl standing there? She's mine, so hands off, I'm going to marry her."

"Which one?" he asked.

I answered, "I only saw one, was someone else with her?"

When we arrived at the CCC camp a short distance away, I quickly unloaded the tools and equipment. The boys needed no coaxing, they were off and hurrying to their tents in moments.

I showered quickly, changed clothes, passed up "chow," and, with "A. G.," went back to the campground where I had seen "the girl," hurrying to get there before anyone else did.

The campers were occupied with their evening meal of potato soup, fried potatoes and onions, and homemade bread brought from home. The tempting aroma of food and coffee over the campfire, and the tangy mountain air fragrant with pine, made me realize how hungry I was, almost to the point of making me forget my purpose in visiting the camp, which definitely was not for food.

We approached the campers and introduced ourselves. The girl I was interested in was Velma Barger, and the redhead was Emma Ropp, her cousin. The girls at first concentrated on their food, trying to ignore us. Velma finally looked up at her mother, saying that she did not like it up here in the mountains and wanted to go home, said for my benefit of course. I looked at her and winked.

"Oh," I said, "you'll get to liking it better around here."

Her mother gave me a stern, unsmiling look, but her father, ignoring the remark, continued eating, perhaps a little faster.

After about two hours of conversation, her mother announced that it was "bed time and visitors should go home."

I was not easily discouraged, and in the following days spent all of my free time there. I was around the family so much that her mother once threatened me with her .22 rifle, which she said she kept "only for varmints," including the two legged kind, and she warned me to stay away from her daughter.

I was not sure if she really meant it and was only having some fun at my expense, so I laughed and said I was not afraid of a "varmint gun." Had I known then that my future bride's mother was a rugged pioneer, who had traveled across the country from Oklahoma to the Pacific Northwest in a covered wagon, I would not have been so bold.

The 1939 Willard Fire

Our relationship continued to grow for about two weeks, even under the watchful eye of her mother, until the day they returned to their home in the Yakima Valley, about 125 miles away. A day later, August 8, 1939, a forest fire ran out of control near Willard, Washington, to the south of us. Eleven squads of fire fighters, including myself, were sent from Camp Skamania for fire fighting duty.

The Willard blaze was the largest and most spectacular fire I ever witnessed. During the hot, dry summer of 1939, it destroyed 13,000 acres, requiring the combined efforts of Camp Skamania, Camp Hemlock near Carson, Washington, and all available local men, as well as other men trucked in from Portland to combat the conflagration.

We set up a field camp near the fire, complete with temporary headquarters, kitchen, and an area for storing and maintaining fire fighting equipment. We slept in sleeping bags under the hemlocks, and washed and shaved with cold water from the small mountain stream that flowed at the edge of camp.

Combating fire is hot, strenuous work, and the men developed hearty appetites. The field kitchen did full justice to the tradition of providing plenty of food for fire fighters (rations were increased by one-third at these times). Cooks kept the cookstoves going day and night, supplying abundant, hot, tasty food twenty-four hours a day to the crews and support personnel. Between regular meal times, hot coffee, sandwiches, and fresh fruit also were sent to men out on the fire lines to help prevent fatigue during the hard and dangerous work.

On one mission, as I transported a crew from the fire lines to the field camp, the wind suddenly blew up and changed direction, causing the blaze to "crown," a situation where fire is blown from the top of one tree to another, sometimes several hundred feet at a time. This is an especially dangerous situation since the flames move so swiftly that a person can easily be trapped.

The fire spread quickly on both sides of the road leaving us with no way out. I had no choice but to drive through the tunnel of fire with my load of "flame tamers" and hope for the best. At one point, sparks from the burning trees ignited the canvas on the truck bed, but it was quickly extinguished by the men. We continued nonstop through the lane of fire to safety.

In another area, flames trapped three water pump operators at the base of a rocky cliff and they almost lost their lives. They were setting up the pumps to water down some hot spots when a sudden shift in the wind caught the nearby timber on fire, trapping them inside a circle of flames. They were saved from burning only by lying down in the small stream that flowed near the base of the cliff. Thus, they had survived by keeping a "cool head." If they had panicked and run from the blaze, in all probability they would have perished.

The "We can take it" boys lived up to their reputation on the Willard burn. Before the fire was under control, however, many fiery battles had to be fought and won, thousands of man-hours had been expended, forty-three miles of firebreaks were built, and, unfortunately, one fire fighter died on the job.

As the blaze burned fiercely at its peak, a crew that had been on the fire line since early morning walked down the mountainside about 5:00 pm to the road, where I was waiting with my truck to transport them back to base camp for much needed food and rest. As they stepped onto the road near my vehicle, one of the men collapsed on the ground. He was about fifty-five years of age and one of the men brought in from Portland to help fight the blaze.

We immediately put our first aid training to use on the stricken fire fighter, trying desperately to revive him. We took turns giving him artificial respiration, until it became certain that all our efforts were futile, that he was, in fact, beyond help, and would not respond to anything we did.

I was especially concerned because he reminded me of my father, who had suffered a heart attack when he was forty-five years old and now was about the same age as the stricken man. As I tried to revive the elderly fire fighter, I thought about how much I missed my Dad.

Another CCC truck had stopped to give assistance. When it was certain that the man had passed away, we wrapped him in a GI blanket and laid his body in the back of my truck. Everyone then boarded the other truck, and I was left alone with the body to transport back to camp.

It was a memorable ride for me. By this time, night had fallen. I was a long way from camp, and there was no one on the road except the dead man and me. I did not feel too good about the situation, having had no experience with this kind of thing before.

When I finally arrived in camp, I discovered that no one wanted to take responsibility for the body. The forester in charge contacted the county coroner, who directed us to bring the deceased man to his office in Stevenson. I set out immediately, arriving at the county seat with the body about 2:00 am in the morning. I left him there with the coroner. It was later determined that the man had died of a heart attack, probably brought on by the prolonged strain and stress of fire fighting.

I looked forward to getting back to camp for food and sleep after a long day's work, compounded by the tragedy of a fire fighter dying and my driving all those hours through the lonely night with his body. The CCC cooks at camp were the "best in the West," and well supplied with choice provisions. It did not take the cook on duty long to broil a thick, juicy steak for me, along with all the trimmings, and in moments I was eating heartily.

A week later, the fire was extinguished and we returned to Camp Skamania. The CCC "axe-perts" had fought and won another battle with the "fire demon."

Wedding "Shivaree"

The romance between Velma and I was "put on hold" by the Willard fire, but, when I returned to Camp Skamania, we picked up where we had left off. We kept in touch through the mail, because in 1939 the few telephones in the Columbia National Forest belonged to the Forest Service and were not available for private use.

Pursuing a romance through correspondence, however, was too slow—much too slow for a twenty-year-old man full of vim and vigor. Charles Niver, the company clerk, was a close friend of mine and owned a 1935 Ford. He and I drove to Velma's hometown of Wapato, a community with a population of about 3,000 on the Yakima Indian Reservation, to see her at every opportunity. Her mother and the rest of the relatives now had accepted me into their family circle, having decided that the 3C's boys were trustworthy and that my intentions were honorable after all.

One evening at camp, I confided in my foreman, Celo Anderson, whom we CCC boys trusted deeply, telling him that I was going to marry that "beautiful girl from the Yakima Valley."

Knowing that he was a bachelor, I was surprised when he heartily approved, jokingly saying that he would pay for the marriage license if and when we were married.

On September 22, 1939, two months after we met in the forest at Smokey Creek, we were married at her parents' home in Wapato. It was a beautiful ceremony they said—I was too excited to notice anything—with many of her relatives and friends present. All of my family was in Georgia, of course, and my CCC buddies could not attend either due to time restrictions or a lack of transportation and money.

I will say here that I was unable to get permission to leave the CCC camp, as it was still fire season. So I did what any determined twenty-year-old red-blooded American would do— I went "over the hill" (AWOL: absent without leave) long enough to help make wedding plans, get married, and enjoy a short honeymoon.

Immediately after the wedding, the "shivaree" began, and it seemed as though the whole town was there joining in on the fun. They hauled me through the Wapato business district on a "Georgia buggy" (wheelbarrow), followed by a cavalcade of automobiles with horns blowing. Velma, surrounded by others in the procession, walked along behind the wheelbarrow pushers.

I managed to avoid a dunking in an irrigation canal, then my bride and I were taken for a drive down country roads along canal and ditch banks until we eluded our pursuers. Finally, after a wedding supper at the local Chinese restaurant, we arrived in the early hours of the morning at Velma's parents' home, where we spent our first night of married life together.

A week later, the company clerk wrote me a letter, asking me to return to camp, saying he would help find a place for Velma and I to live nearby. After borrowing a tent and other camping equipment from her father, and with the help of the CCC boys, we moved to the Smokey Creek Campground where we had first met. According to regulations, newly married men could finish out their current hitch in the CCC, but they could not reenlist after that time.

We stayed there until the company moved back to winter quarters at Camp Sunset a few days later. Then we rented a cabin at Horseshoe Falls on the East Fork of the Lewis River, located a couple miles west of Camp Sunset. We later moved into a small house in Yacolt, where we lived until I was discharged from the Civilian Conservation Corps on December 21, 1939.

CCC Entertainment: A Minstrel Show and Beer

As busy as we were during the summer of 1938, patrolling for and fighting forest blazes and doing fire presuppression work, we did manage to produce a minstrel show and presented it on stage at the Trout Lake High School. It was written and directed by an enrollee, "Cotton" McDermott, the assistant educational adviser, who used a cast made up entirely of CCC boys. We spent all of our spare time rehearsing the show until the big night finally arrived.

At curtain time, the auditorium was filled to capacity with Trout Lake residents and CCC boys not confined to camp for fire or other duty. The comedy was well received by the large audience. It was a welcomed diversion from the still lingering social and economic woes of the depression. Jobs remained hard to find, and cash was as "scarce as hen's teeth," especially money for entertainment.

The only "fatalities" of the performance were the stage curtains, which were soiled with makeup used by the performers. They had to undergo a professional cleaning and repair job. And, two or three CCC boys, who were not in the show, became "a little intoxicated," causing a commotion after the performance was over. A good time was had by all, and the next day it was "work as usual" for the 3C's boys.

Occasionally in those summer months of 1938 and 1939, a small group of lads, including myself, would stop at Ice Cave when traveling between Camp Skamania and Trout Lake. It was located on National Forest land about eight miles south of the Smokey Creek camp and only a few hundred feet off the main traveled road. Ice Cave is a lava tube about 600 feet long, but its roof is just several feet under the surface of the ground.

Its icy floor, icicles, and large masses of drip ice form during the winter months when moisture freezes. Much of this ice remains throughout the year. Early settlers were familiar with Ice Cave, and, no doubt, Indians knew about it many years before the whites arrived. It supplied ice for the Columbia River towns of Hood River and The Dalles in Oregon in pioneer days.

We stopped at Ice Cave at every opportunity, armed with beer purchased at the Trout Lake Hotel. Although it was against Army and Forest Service regulations to have alcoholic beverages in camp or CCC vehicles, we always found a way to acquire it and keep it without getting caught. Beer not consumed often was hidden in the cool recesses of the cave, where it remained until our next opportunity came along to visit the cavern and polish it off. It was exciting to explore Ice Cave.

In August 1985, one of my sons and I visited the cavern and it still is as cool and icy today as it was the first time I stopped there in 1938. We also drove up to the site of old Camp Skamania on the banks of Smokey Creek. The stream, clear and cold, still gurgles over the rocks as it did when the camp was located there, just a few feet from where the mess hall and kitchen once stood. I still can point out the exact spot in the stream where I hid beer to keep it cold and out of sight of other thirsty boys.

CCC tug of war. As might be expected in this era, Blacks normally served in segregated units, mostly in the South. Sometimes, however, a few Black enrollees were assigned to what were otherwise all white companies, including camps in the Pacific Northwest. *Manuscripts, Archives, and Special Collections, Washington State University Library, Pullman*

Chapter Six

CAMP COUGAR AND MT. ST. HELENS

Another day, another dollar—
a million days and I'll be a millionaire!

Popular saying by CCC boys

During much of the winter of 1938-1939, I was stationed at a side camp at Cougar, Washington, serving as a truck driver for a crew stringing telephone lines. At the time, there were few telephones in that part of the old Columbia National Forest. Consequently, 3C's boys were sent there to alleviate the problem, which we did in record time. Forest Service officials were grateful to us for installing a long overdue communication system, as it greatly benefited the agency in its forestry work, especially during fire season.

The Cougar side camp was small. It stood in a beautiful setting on the banks of the Lewis River, a few miles upstream from Yale, Washington, near the base of beautiful, ice crowned Mt. St. Helens. The camp consisted of only a few facilities—a barracks, a combination mess hall and kitchen, a tool shed, and a small water-cooled structure near the kitchen to keep food fresh.

The water-cooled structure was the result of the "We can do it" ingenuity of the CCC boys. Water was piped to it from a spring on the nearby mountainside. The roof and sides of the walk-in cooler were covered with burlap. A sprinkling system was placed on the roof to keep the structure wet with the cold springwater, maintaining a cool temperature inside to preserve perishable food items.

Other ongoing projects included building fire trails and improving existing forest roads and trails. Our small crew consisted of a foreman, leadman, assistant leadman, and about twenty-five boys, including a cook, KP, and one other truck driver besides myself. Good meals were provided in all of the camps in which I stayed, but the food at Camp Cougar was superior.

It was prepared by "Baby Face," an enrollee who took great pride in his work. A farm boy from the South, he had enrolled in the CCC, hoping to fulfill his dream of becoming a great chef. Once in the CCC, he quickly was nicknamed "Baby Face" because he had the beardless face and innocent expression of a youngster.

Side camps received more provisions per man than the main camps, making it possible for them to serve choice foods and treats more often. As the number one truck driver and a good friend of the cook, I had access to the kitchen anytime I wanted for a snack or meal, and, consequently, I fared well, even after regular "chow" hours.

Playing pinochle was a popular pastime in the long evenings after supper, with two or three games being played simultaneously. After working up an appetite playing cards, we often fired up the woodburning range, grabbed food from the cooler, and enjoyed a "midnight snack."

One weekend when the smelt run was at its peak in the Columbia River, we went "smelting." Using a net attached to the end of a long pole, in a short time we had dipped up enough smelt for all of the boys at camp. We also fished for trout in the Lewis River, but with limited success.

We often hiked the mountain trails on weekends, crossing the river on a "swinging" footbridge located a short distance above camp. There were signs posted at each end warning pedestrians not to walk in unison on the bridge. It was possible to start a rhythmic, rocking motion that could undermine the bridge's internal support, causing it to collapse into the river, taking hikers with it. On one occasion, a group of enrollees walked to Spirit Lake, located many miles away on the north side of Mt. St. Helens. Others hiked up the slopes of the mountain as far as possible, which was not very far in the winter due to the deep snowpack.

We were in excellent physical condition due to the type of work we did, the well balanced meals, and the fresh air and regular sleep (being young also helped), so hiking was never a problem with us. If we wanted to go somewhere and transportation was unavailable, without hesitation we walked.

On off duty weekends, I drove the boys to Vancouver. On the way, I always let a few boys off at the small towns of Woodland and Amboy, where they attended social events or visited. When I returned, they were waiting at the appointed place for a ride back to the barracks, where a warm bunk awaited them. Several boys from Camp Cougar later married girls they dated and settled in the area.

Memories of Our Dog, "Baby"

Many CCC camps kept pets for mascots, and Camp Cougar was no exception. Our mascot was a small dog named "Baby" by the boys. She was friendly to everyone, and got very excited when we returned to camp, greeting us with gyrations, eager barks, and a "smile."

No one knew for sure or would admit where she came from, but one popular rumor was that she "followed" one of the CCC lads to camp and "liked it so much she decided to make it her home."

She slept in the barracks with us, and we fed her "people food" from the mess hall. Her welfare was jealously watched over by her adopted family.

She was a trusting and friendly dog, and liked to play. She always was ready for a good romp, often following along when we went hiking or exploring along the river and in the woods. She quickly learned the "chow" call, which a cook sounded by striking a metal pipe against an old brake drum (we called this makeshift gong the "gut hammer"). "Baby" would run to the mess hall as fast as her short legs could carry her.

One Saturday night, she was not in her usual place in the barracks. We assumed that she was off somewhere with one of the enrollees. But, when she was still absent the next day at noon, and with all the boys accounted for, we were afraid that she had been "dognapped" or hurt in some manner. We started to search the area, first among the buildings, and then outward from the camp and along the river, while calling out to each other to keep in touch.

Finally, after searching for several hours, one of the boys, "Big Foot" Johnson, yelled, "Here she is down by the river, but I'm afraid we're too late."

We hastened to where he had found her body near the shore, drowned in the cold waters of the Lewis River. No one ever knew how it occurred, but in all probability she had tried to get too friendly with a black bear or some other wild animal and was fatally attacked near the water's edge. We buried her near the camp, very much saddened by her untimely demise.

Ole Peterson

One of the most interesting persons I ever met was Ole Peterson, a man nearly eighty years of age who lived in a cabin near camp. Tall and lanky, Ole was friendly, easygoing, and happy with his unusual lifestyle. He grazed a few cattle in the locality, made home brew for his own consumption, chopped firewood for fuel, and kept a collection of old automobiles in his yard.

The spring that supplied water for the CCC camp also served Ole's cabin, with the overflow running in a small ditch past his place. Close to the cabin, he dug out a short section of the stream to make it deeper, and built a shelter over it to keep wild animals (and CCC boys) out, while keeping an ample supply of "home brew" submerged there to stay cool.

On many long winter evenings, we gathered at his cabin to listen to his interesting tales and hilarious jokes. The stories he told about hunting and fishing in the Mt. St. Helens area were spiced up with a few off-color quips about his "bullhorn" walking canes, and usually brought on a "Little Audrey" joke, the first of several "sick jokes" by one of the boys. Ole's wit and geniality made him a favorite with the CCC boys, and he was always available for conversation or a story.

Ole never threw out newspapers, magazines, or catalogs— no one knew the reason why—until he had them stacked to the ceiling of his cabin. In the mid 1940s, the cabin was destroyed by fire, and Ole was severely burned. He was taken to a hospital, where he died a short time later.

Although he lived alone and was very independent, in the last days of his life Ole accepted help from friends, who chopped and hauled wood for him. He always will be remembered by the CCC boys that knew him. He left an indelible impression on the young men serving at Camp Cougar.

I served in or visited a number of camps during the three years that I was in the CCC. One of the most memorable was Camp Cougar, in the shadow of Mt. St. Helens, even though I was there only a short time.

Discharge, December 21, 1939

Upon leaving the CCC, I worked at any job available—as an auto mechanic, machinist, or truck driver—followed by eighteen months stateside service in the Army toward the end of World War II.

Afterward, Velma and I, now with three small children (Ronald Edwin, Carole Ann, and Edwin Wayne), moved to the Yakima Valley. Again, I worked at various jobs, including two years with the Bureau of Indian Affairs, followed by sixteen years

with the Wapato School District, where I was a "jack of all trades."
I was a bus driver, electrician, plumber, heating technician, and
took on any other duties necessary to maintain the six schools in
the district.

In October 1969, I accepted a position as Building Superintendent with the City of Yakima. This was the most interesting
and rewarding employment of my career—one in which I utilized
all the experience and skills that I had acquired over the years.
I enjoyed not only the challenging technical and administrative
aspects of the job, but also the interaction with City Hall officials
and the public.

During this time, I remained involved in various social and
church activities, as well as other volunteer tasks, especially with
the youth of the community. After retiring from the City of Yakima
on January 30, 1981, however, I had more time to contribute to
volunteer projects, including the local food bank, Red Cross, jury
duty, the Civil Service Board, and others.

I particularly enjoyed helping young people, remembering
my own youth and the difficulties of "growing up" during the
Great Depression. I was fortunate to have had a great organization, the CCC, and caring people to help me through those hard
years. I am of the firm opinion that today's youth will not fail
themselves, their nation, or their civic duties. I believe, however,
that we, the older adults, fail them if we do not provide firm,
positive leadership and direction.

In August 1980, I helped found and was first president of
Yakima Valley Chapter #39, of the National Association of
Civilian Conservation Corps Alumni (our charter is dated September 1, 1980). We greatly enjoy our "CCC boys'" camaraderie at our
monthly dinner meetings. Friendships formed in the CCC have
lasted a lifetime.

THE CCC STORY

"Soil soldiers" in the Palouse country. In the Lewiston [Idaho] CCC District and the Fort George Wright [Spokane] CCC District, camps near such towns as Dayton, Pomeroy, Genesee, Pullman, Moscow, Davenport, and Walla Walla did extensive soil conservation work on wheatlands. Many additional companies did forestry work in the mountains of eastern Washington, northeast Oregon, the Idaho Panhandle, and western Montana. *Manuscripts, Archives, and Special Collections, Washington State University Library, Pullman*

Chapter Seven

THE CCC IN THE PACIFIC NORTHWEST

Show me the way to go home,
I'm tired and I want to go to bed,
I've been a 'fightin fire in the CCC,
My beans I have been fed.
Wherever I may roam,
On land or sea or foam,
You can always hear me
Singing this song,
Show me the way to go home.

"Show Me the Way To Go Home,"
Fort Lewis CCC songbook, 1934

Reassignment from one locality to another, or even to a different region of the country, was an adventure experienced by many CCC boys, especially those lads serving more than a single six month enlistment. While some preferred to remain in CCC camps in their home state, where they could be close to their family and friends (especially sweethearts!) and familiar surroundings, others wanted to see new places and seek different experiences.

A book could be written about the hundreds of CCC camps in the Pacific Northwest alone. It probably is impossible, in fact, to determine exactly how many there were between 1933 and 1942, due to the constant shuffling of companies to different localities, and the frequent arrival of new, out of state contingents, usually from the East.

Also throughout this nine year period, companies were disbanded and reconstituted, or enrollees from two or more camps were brought together to form new companies. In addition to the "main" camps, great numbers of subsidiary "side" or "spike" camps were established to be close to specific projects or danger zones during fire season.

In 1939, for example, a group of "wandering" CCC boys from New York, serving as Company 1297, was transferred to Washington. They were assigned to Bureau of Reclamation summer camps at Kachess Lake, Bumping Lake, and Keechelus Lake in Washington's central Cascades, and moved to Camp Zillah, near Yakima, for the winter months.

Two tall columns of mortared native stone, inscribed by the enrollees with the words "CCC Company 1297 Nov 7 1939 AD" and "CCC Camp Zillah BR-58 Nov 7 1939 AD," were erected at the gates of the main camp, located two miles from Zillah. They now stand alone in a fruit orchard, the only physical reminders that this once was the site of a CCC camp—the "home away from home" of young men from far off New York.

Following are brief descriptions of a representative number of camps, as well as some recollections by enrollees, illustrating the Civilian Conservation Corps' accomplishments in the Pacific Northwest. Keep in mind that this is by no means a complete list of all the CCC camps in the region.

J. D. McReynolds at the Naches and Goldendale Camps

"When I was eighteen years old, I was living in Ahtanum, a little town southwest of Yakima, Washington. I had no job and no money, so I joined the 3C's. I was assigned to Company 932, a forestry camp at Naches, Washington, where we built camp-grounds in the Chinook Pass and White Pass areas of the Cascades.

"I also helped construct fire trails and participated in other projects. Some of the boys worked in the 'sign shop,' making the handsome signs commonly seen at the entrances to camp-grounds. We also had a carpentry shop, and a big swimming pool out in front of the barracks.

"Camp Naches was quite nice. When winter came, we went out and cut our own firewood, and hauled it to camp to burn in our barracks stoves [more will be said about Camp Naches shortly].

"When the Naches camp was closed down, I transferred to Company 945, stationed at the Goldendale fairgrounds in Klickitat County. It was a soil conservation camp, and the work we did there was quite different from that at Camp Naches, which had been a forestry camp.

"We sloped the ditch banks on the farms in the area, trying to keep the soil from washing away. Today, as you drive into Goldendale from the Yakima direction, you can see some of our work just outside of town along the creek, where we laid riprap of flat rock along the banks. It is pretty much overgrown with brush now, however."

Now to return to the story of Company 932 and Camp Naches. The company first built, and originally was assigned to, Camp Nile, located on Nile Creek, a tributary of the Naches River. On May 16, 1933, twenty-five "Washington men" from Fort Lewis arrived there, and, four days later, an additional twenty-five men from Naches and Yakima were enlisted to help construct the camp, which Company 932 then occupied for six months.

At first, the company was run by noncommissioned officers of the U. S. Army. When the enrollees became proficient enough to administer themselves, these regular Army "noncoms" re-turned to their post. More recruits were enrolled, until the company reached its full strength of 250 men, the majority of them from west of the Cascades.

In the fall of 1933, Company 932 moved west of the mountains to Camp Cherry Valley, located east of Seattle near Fall City, and spent the winter. In the spring, they returned east of the Cascades again to build Camp Naches, F-70, which the company occupied in May 1934. Over the years, they continued to improve the facilities at the camp.

Among their duties was the construction of a dozen buildings at the Naches Ranger Station, as well as three portable structures for side camps. Enrollees developed campgrounds, built camp stoves, tables, and benches, strung telephone and power lines, erected lookouts, cut trails and firebreaks, constructed a horse barn, and established their own sawmill at the camp. They battled forest fires—both in the local area and as far away as Oregon, where, in the fall of 1936, forty-eight men from Company 932 spent a month fighting fire.

They built a one-half mile trail to Boulder Cave, a four-hundred feet long cavern that probably was occupied by Indians as much as 8,000 years ago. Boulder Cave is located along the Naches River, near Cliffdell on the Chinook Pass highway. A picnic area also was constructed next to the start of the trail. (After a half-century of use, the trail recently was renovated by the Youth Conservation Corps, which also helped build a retaining wall leading to the cave.)

The construction of Enderud Hall, the educational and recreational structure at Camp Naches, was a major accomplishment for the enrollees. The building, with its fine dance floor, natural stone fireplace, stage, movie projection room, library, and classrooms, was considered one of the finest facilities of its kind in the Fort Lewis CCC District. It was provided with Ping-pong tables, piano, pool tables, radio, and tables for writing, checkers, and chess.

Later, in the spring of 1937, the enrollees began constructing a swimming pool at the camp. When completed, it provided many hours of enjoyment for the enlistees. The boys donated their time to excavate a hole for the pool, which was cribbed with logs. A large amount of water was needed to fill it and to keep it filled, because seepage was lost through the log cribbing. When it became necessary to change the water, it was pumped out and used to irrigate the lawn and shrubbery.

A waterwheel and fish screen were fabricated and installed in the water supply channel to keep fish from entering the pool. Water flowing through the channel rotated the waterwheel—its chain and sprocket drive, which turned the fish screen, blocked entry to fish, redirecting them back to the river with a flow of water specifically provided for that purpose. (I visited the site on July 19, 1986, finding it still in excellent operating condition.)

Recreational and athletic activities always were important at Camp Naches. There were facilities for badminton, tennis, croquet, horseshoes, and basketball, and fishing and hiking were enjoyed by many enrollees. Excursions to Mt. Rainier were organized in the summer, while weekly trips to Yakima for recreational and home visits were provided year around.

Educational opportunities were many and varied, with classes in typing, music, dramatics, English, carpentry, auto mechanics, welding, photography, cooking, baking, and other subjects. In addition, many boys enrolled in correspondence courses. Library management skills also were taught to enrollees so they could help care for the camp library of more than 2,000 volumes.

Some other good "morale builders" were the twenty member Drum and Bugle Corps, and the company newspaper, the *War Whoop*, published twice monthly and distributed to all members of Company 932. It was given a three star rating by *Happy Days*, the official national CCC newspaper published in Washington, D.C.

Boys at Camp Naches having artistic ability decorated the mess hall with murals, which gained some notoriety. For example, the August 23, 1935, edition of the *Saltwater Seagull*, published at Camp Saltwater on the east side of Puget Sound, between Tacoma and Seattle, reported: "CCC Camp Naches has the distinction of having the Camp's Mess Hall walls painted with artistic pictures depicting CCC life. Canvas is now being prepared

Fort Lewis CCC District, 1937. At this time there were twenty-nine active camps; two years before there were a record fifty-four main camps. *Official Annual–Fort Lewis District Civilian Conservation Corps Ninth Corps Area, 1937*

for more of this ambitious work. When finished, the pictures will adorn the booth at the Western Washington Fair at Puyallup September 16-22, 1935."

One outstanding project undertaken by Camp Naches was the development of the American River ski bowl and ski lodge. The beautiful and spacious lodge was constructed to withstand the harsh winter environment of the mountains, particularly the heavy snowfall. Completed on November 13, 1935, it was the most popular ski bowl in the locality until the White Pass ski area opened many years later.

Decades later, in November 1983, several CCC veterans who helped build the lodge—Ken Sprague, Leonard Sherry, Jack Green, and others who still live in the region—gathered for a reunion at the ski bowl. Several months later, in June 1984, a crew of CCC veterans led by Leonard Sherry and David Rust reroofed the structure. The old shakes that they replaced were the same ones that had been nailed onto the roof in 1935. The new shakes were handmade by David Rust at the site of old Camp Naches.

The lodge stands in the evergreens about three miles off State Route 410. It remains in excellent condition, and is utilized by groups from around the region throughout the year.

Veterans of Company 932 and other camps gathered at the lodge on July 14, 1984, to celebrate the fiftieth anniversary of Camp Naches. Some alumni came from as far away as New Jersey to attend the reunion and picnic. It was the largest gathering of CCC alumni in central Washington since the CCC disbanded in 1942.

Camp Ginkgo

In October 1935, Company 935 moved from Camp Saltwater, situated south of Seattle, to Camp Ginkgo, which had been authorized for construction along the Columbia River at Vantage. The semiarid climate contrasted markedly with the milder and wetter conditions west of the Cascades to which the boys were accustomed. In central Washington, the summer months are hot and dry, and the winters cold and snowy.

It was a landscape of sagebrush, greasewood, sand, and rocks, instead of evergreen forests and lush undergrowth. Here, in these dry hills, a wide variety of wildlife thrived year around—deer, elk, coyote, the ubiquitous jackrabbit, ravens, hawks, and, that great national symbol, the bald eagle. From spring to fall, there were lizards, scorpions, gopher snakes, and, that lethal western inhabitant, the rattlesnake.

Interesting as this semiarid land was, with its numerous songbirds and other wildlife, great rolling hills, and colorful scenery, there were some boys who were not happy and went "over the hill" (AWOL) and did not return.

The main projects at Camp Ginkgo focused on the development of Ginkgo Petrified Forest State Park and its museum. As soon as they were settled into their new camp, the CCC lads began work on the park facilities, and, along with a crew of Works Progress Administration (WPA) men, began erecting the museum on a bluff commanding a majestic view of the Columbia River and the vertical cliffs lining its banks.

In addition, other structures were built near the museum, as well as at a location about three miles from the river, where new trails were cut and petrified logs were uncovered for viewing by park visitors. The museum building and other facilities were hand built with native stone.

The main attraction in this sizeable park were fossils of some 200 species of trees and plants from a forest habitat that existed here some ten million years ago. The trees were entombed by molten lava and petrified. One species in particular, the ginkgo, is noteworthy for its numerous fossils found in the Vantage locality.

Through the millennia, ginkgo trees have entirely disappeared from the forests of the world. They only survived in the Orient, where for centuries priests and monks domesticated and preserved them as ornamental trees in temple gardens. Today, of course, the ginkgo has been reintroduced into the United States, and several thriving ginkgo trees now stand by the park museum, where they were planted and cultivated by park employees.

Camp Ginkgo enrollees attended dances and various social activities at nearby Quincy, or they went to Ellensburg for movies, dances, or to visit friends. They participated in football, basketball, boxing, and baseball, competing with other CCC camps and local teams, while winning many contests.

In March 1936, the camp's bimonthly newspaper, *Petrified Paragraphs*, featured one of the camp's star athletes in its "Ginkgo All-American" sports section. He was Arthur "Powerhouse" Abbott, a graduate of West Seattle High School, where he had been a tackle on the football team, and an ace shot-putter and the captain of the track team. Another "Ginkgo All-American" was Thomas Cassidy, a former football star at Franklin High School in Seattle, who also was a great shortstop on the baseball team.

The February 26, 1936, edition of *Petrified Paragraphs* reported an inspection by Major Ralph Hirsch, who gave the camp a rating of "excellent plus." The enrollee reporting the story, however, noted that the boys were disappointed, and would not be satisfied until the camp was rated "superior." They planned to continue their efforts until that goal was achieved.

All across the nation, talented young writers and artists worked on CCC camp newspaper staffs. The camp artist for *Petrified Paragraphs*, Paul A. Lawrence, was typical. Altogether, he served two years in various CCC camps, as an artist for the *Saltwater Seagull* at Camp Saltwater and for *Petrified Paragraphs* at Camp Ginkgo, and as the editor of *Progress*, the Camp Conconully newspaper.

After his service in the CCC, Lawrence eventually wrote several books on health topics, including *Lomi-Lomi Hawaiian Massage, In Praise of Chocolate, Manipulative Therapy Massage,* and *Food Will Be the Medicine of the Future.* He also later wrote and published an interesting and informative book, *Remembering the CCC* (1983), which includes illustrations, etchings, and sketches.

Company 935 disbanded April 12, 1936, and the enrollees were sent to fill vacancies in other camps. Coming in as a replacement was Company 3224, from Camp Dix, New Jersey.

The boys from New York and New Jersey continued making improvements in the state park.

Beacon Rock State Park

Company 5480, formed at Fort Oglethorpe, Georgia, on October 8, 1936, consisted of an eight man cadre and 142 enrollees, all from Tennessee. For some reason, the recruiters selected the largest young men out of a group of 600 enrollees in the conditioning camp to fill out the company roster.

At first, Company 5480 did work for the Soil Conservation Service at Camp Winfield Scott, SCS-8, Church Road, Virginia. While working on local erosion control projects, the boys' friendly and caring attitude engendered a lasting friendship between them and the residents of the area.

In this period, some enrollees from other southern states came in as replacements. Under the supervision of the company's athletic director, the basketball team won many games, while the boys on the baseball team, known as the "Clowns," made a name for themselves playing other CCC camps and local "civilian" teams.

Several enrollees also formed a musical group known as "Jimmie Driver's Tennessee Playboys," with Jesse Hesson as vocalist. They attracted wide attention through weekly broadcasts over radio station WPHR in Petersburg, Virginia. The group was an instant hit. In came a flood of invitations to perform at dances, school and church socials, and other events.

A year later, however, orders came for Company 5480 to leave Virginia and proceed to Camp Beacon Rock, SP-13, near Skamania, Washington. They boarded the train on October 6, 1937, and arrived at Camp Beacon Rock at 5:30 am on October 11, having traveled 3,600 miles in five days and nights through thirteen states.

Beacon Rock is located in the spectacular Columbia River Gorge, about thirty-five miles east of Vancouver. The great stone monolith, for which the park is named, apparently is an eroded volcanic core that rises 850 feet high. The Lewis and Clark expedition first spotted it on October 31, 1805, at which time Captain William Clark named it "Beacon Rock."

Within a short time after arriving at their new home in the "Far West," Company 5480 began developing the property into one of the finest state parks in the Pacific Northwest. Under the supervision of parks' personnel, camp sites were established, hiking trails were cut, and fireplaces, tables, shelters, and other picnic and recreational facilities were constructed.

One major project was the erection of several permanent buildings, built with timbers and native stone. The rustic, yet handsome, design of these structures aptly expressed the pride and craftsmanship of the CCC boys and their "we can do it better" spirit. A half century later, the accomplishments of the CCC boys remain very much in evidence in the 425 acre park. Still present are camp facilities, as well as stone and timbered structures erected by the CCC.

The park's main recreational attraction—the spectacular 4,500 feet long Beacon Rock trail, was cut out of the monolith's cliffs and zigzags to its summit. The trail dates from the 1910s, but the CCC helped make improvements as needed. Today, an extensive system of handrails is provided for the safety of hikers.

From the top, hikers gain a spectacular panorama of the broad Columbia River and its islands, as well as the evergreen forests and rugged cliffs of the gorge. Another excellent hiking trail extends northward from the park to the summit of Mt. Hamilton, which overlooks the Columbia along many miles of its course. (Other CCC companies developed parks on the Oregon side of the gorge too, such as at Eagle Creek near Bonneville Dam.)

Camp Hemlock

At Camp Hemlock, F-40, located near Carson, Washington, about twenty-five miles northeast of Beacon Rock, Company 944 worked on a variety of projects in the old Columbia National Forest. The company, consisting of boys from the Evergreen State, was organized May 15, 1933, at Fort Lewis.

The next day, they set out for the Hemlock Ranger Station, arriving shortly after noon. After setting up a temporary camp, they began constructing permanent buildings, which were ready for occupation on June 12, 1933, less than a month after the new company had arrived there. Also located here were the Wind River tree nursery and the Wind River branch of the Pacific Northwest Experiment Station.

Fifteen days after their arrival, snag falling commenced, and, on the next day after that, work began on a permanent water system. In less than a month, all of the enrollees, with the exception of the necessary camp "overhead," had been turned over to the Forest Service to work on various projects, including downing snags, planting trees, constructing and repairing roads, trails, and telephone lines, maintaining trucks and equipment, and performing lookout and fire guard duty. At the camp, landscaping work and sign making were ongoing operations. Company 944, of course, also fought forest fires when the need arose.

The development of Government Mineral Springs Campground, located several miles north of Camp Hemlock up the Wind River, was an important summer project. Camping sites, stone fireplaces, and a water system that provided a faucet to each camping unit were constructed here.

In 1935, the enrollees built Trout Creek Dam, which was one of the largest hydroelectric projects ever completed solely by a CCC company, and one of the first to include a fish ladder. Constructed on Trout Creek near Camp Hemlock, the 183 feet long dam supplied power for more than thirty Forest Service shops, residences, offices, and storage buildings. Following the completion of the dam, they constructed a double-hinged arch bridge made of wood timbers, spanning the small lake formed by the dam (it was replaced by a modern bridge in 1975).

In 1936, the boys built a handsome office building for the Wind River Experiment Station, and started construction of a Forest Service regional training school; two structures were completed in 1936 and 1937, and used for training rangers and supervisors, and other facilities were added as needed. The prime duty at Hemlock in the summer fire season was to protect the forests along the Washington side of the Columbia River Gorge. For this reason, it was an ideal location for a Forest Service fire training school.

Camp Hemlock always remained the permanent home for Company 944, except during the summer of 1934 when the enrollees were moved twelve miles west to Camp Lookout Mountain. The boys were not only efficient in their work, but also excelled in athletics. In the 1933-1934 season, for example, the "Red Rangers" basketball team won sixteen games, while losing eight. In the summer of 1935, the softball team won eleven games while losing only a single contest. In the summer of 1936, the track team won the district meet, and a football squad was organized at the camp that fall.

Camp Hemlock, because of its many activities, was noted for being one of the most versatile of any of the CCC camps in the region. It was also one of the few camps occupied by the same unit, Company 944, from the date of its inception until it was disbanded in 1942.

Robert Smith, an enrollee who served two enlistments at Camp Hemlock, remembers running foot races to the top of "Bunker Hill," a mountain north of camp. While serving there, "Bob" learned leathercraft, sign painting, and sandblasting. Like so many other alumni, he has many fond memories of Camp Hemlock, as well as of the camp he served in at Metaline Falls in northeast Washington, where he spent much of his free time ice skating in the cold winter months.

Camp Lower Cispus

Company 2919, F-34, was a "moving camp." It originally was known as Company 1639, F-35. Formed in the spring of 1933, it at first was largely composed of LEM's, with thirty "junior" enrollees brought in from Missouri. They set up camp four miles from Randle on the Cispus Road.

Companies 697 and 933, from Fort Lewis, also were active along the lower and upper stretches, respectively, of the Cispus

River in this period. The Cispus is a tributary of the broad Cowlitz River watershed that drains the western Cascades between Mt. Rainier to the north, and Mt. St. Helens and Mt. Adams in the south.

In the fall, the company moved up to Packwood, seventeen miles east of Randle, and remained there in a winter camp, working in the Packwood Ranger District. In April 1934, the company moved again, this time to a site named Camp Upper Cispus on the Cispus River, about twenty-five miles southeast of Randle. Camp Upper Cispus was the headquarters of the company during the summer of 1934, and afterward was used as a side camp during each fire season.

In the autumn of 1934, the company returned to Packwood, remaining there a year. In October 1935, the boys moved to their final location at Camp Lower Cispus on the Cispus River, about eleven miles from Randle (here, two years earlier, Company 933 had established the first "permanent" CCC camp in the Fort Lewis District).

By this time, the unit designation was changed to Company 2919, Camp F-34. The company was destined to remain at Lower Cispus until the CCC was disbanded in 1942. The company's principal side camp, established in 1934, was located about thirty miles southeast of Randle on the shore of a beautiful lake at the headwaters of Sheep Creek (4,300 feet elevation). An unforgettable sight for the CCC boys was majestic Mt. Adams, only seven miles distant, mirrored in the waters of the lake.

Camp Lower Cispus was in an area known as the Cispus burn, where in 1902 a great forest fire roared over the Cascades from the east and into the Cispus Valley. The conflagration was one of the most destructive in Pacific Northwest history, burning approximately 500,000 acres and resulting in a tremendous loss of natural resources.

Of the many outstanding projects undertaken and completed by Company 2919, many are still being used a half century later. They established campgrounds at such locations as La Wis Wis (just outside of the southeast entrance to Mt. Rainier National Park), at North Fork (near the mouth of the North Cispus River), and at Takhlakh Lake and Council Lake (both just northwest of Mt. Adams). South of the Cispus River, they constructed the McCoy Creek road leading to mines in that watershed. They strung telephone lines and erected lookout stations over the entire Randle Ranger District, and cut more than 200 miles of trails, as well as numerous firebreaks.

An outstanding act of heroism was performed by Vernon Peterson, a member of the company, when a woman was swept away, and, unfortunately, drowned in a branch of the Cispus River. A group of men, including Peterson, were trucked to the scene to assist in recovering the victim.

He descended into the river canyon, plunged into the strong current. Reaching the woman's body, he held her for forty-five minutes until ropes were lowered. Peterson's feet were severely cut on the rocks. Upon his arrival at the camp, he was sent to the infirmary, where he spent two weeks recuperating from the ordeal.

The Cispus Environmental Learning Center now occupies the former site of Camp Lower Cispus, and is used by some 9,000 school children and adults each year. The "Sasquatch Lair," complete with a stone fireplace, is the only original building left from the CCC era, however. It is in excellent condition, and generally is used as the staff and counselors' lounge.

Company 4786 at Ostrich Bay, Mt. Rainier National Park, and Deception Pass State Park

Company 4786, consisting of boys from Missouri, was formed from Casual Company G at Fort Leavenworth, Kansas, on October 11, 1936. After staying a few days at Fort Leavenworth, the company was sent by train to Camp Ostrich Bay, Washington, located just a few miles west of Bremerton and the U. S. Navy's Puget Sound Naval Shipyard.

Camp Ostrich Bay had been established earlier by the CCC, merely a quarter mile from Puget Sound. The camp stood within the boundaries of the Naval Ammunition Depot, which was surrounded by a high security fence. Stored at the depot were thousands of tons of military explosives and ammunition, all under strict surveillance by U. S. Marine Corps guards.

Living in the Puget Sound country at a military base was, of course, a unique experience for the carefree lads, who were accustomed to the great open spaces of the prairies. The CCC boys, however, quickly became accustomed to the new environment, enjoying their six month stay there.

For the first time in their lives, they saw merchant freighters, U. S. Navy destroyers, submarines, and battleships, and, occasionally, huge ocean liners cruising the azure waters of Puget Sound. They enjoyed organized field trips in this new and different locality, as well as ferry rides and sailing on the sound. They spent much of their free time collecting shell specimens on the beaches, and watching naval shipping arriving and leaving at Bremerton's great dry docks.

Company 4786's main duties were the construction of naval air bases at Keyport and Sandpoint. These hardworking boys from the "show me" state quickly earning a reputation as efficient laborers.

In late spring, however, they received orders to move to a new location. Consequently, on May 10, 1937, the company boarded trucks and was hauled to Tahoma Creek in the southwest corner of Mt. Rainier National Park. When the enrollees arrived, they were fascinated by the spectacular scenery, which was so different from the maritime environment of Ostrich Bay. Here, lofty peaks lifted their snow crowned heads on either side of the camp. Farther up the canyon stood 14,410 feet high Mt. Rainier, glistening white above the clouds—the highest peak in the Pacific Northwest and the focus of the greatest glacial system on any single peak in the lower forty-eight United States.

Again, the adventurous Missourians were experiencing a complete change of scenery. They quickly adjusted to their new life in the mountains. Here, within the boundaries of the park, cougar, mountain goat, deer, black bear, and numerous other types of wildlife roamed through the forests of Douglas fir, hemlock, and cedar. Trout abounded in the clear streams, and the beautiful mountains, lakes, and rivers beckoned hikers and amateur photographers from the camp.

Because of the site's remoteness, education ranked high for the enrollees of Company 4786. A woodworking shop was built from scrap lumber and other materials acquired by "midnight requisition." Enrollees crafted furniture, footlockers, and other keepsakes. Many boys also took correspondence courses, as well as photography and other academic classes held in the camp.

Despite the near idyllic setting, misfortune did strike. John Ferris, while returning from a Sunday outing on nearby Mt. Wow, slipped and slid about seventy feet to his death beneath an "ice cap." It took his "brother enrollees" four hours to recover and return Ferris' body to camp. The enrollees drew ever closer together to help each other get through their time of sorrow.

The men's duties were many, including trail building, clearing and repairing roads struck by wintertime avalanches, stringing telephone lines, and erecting lodge facilities. Company 4786, however, was not destined to remain at Mt. Rainier long enough to complete the numerous projects started in the park.

After only six months of service in the Cascades, orders were received to transfer the company to Camp Deception Pass, SP-3, located north of Oak Harbor, Washington. On November 15, 1937, they again were on the move, aptly living up to the title of the company's newspaper, *The Missouri Wanderer*.

Deception Pass State Park, situated along the spectacularly scenic channel separating Whidbey and Fidalgo islands, was similar in setting to that of Camp Ostrich Bay; except, of course, there were no Marine guards, ammunition stores, or security fences. The camp had been established by a previous contingent of CCC boys. It stood in the forest adjacent to the shore of Whidbey Island's Cornet Bay, just south of the narrow channel of Deception Pass.

The enrollees enjoyed returning to Puget Sound, where they spent much of their spare time watching passing ships and ferries, beachcombing and spying on the locality's great number of seabirds, and scrambling through the forests and over the cliffs. From here, it was only a short distance to Anacortes. There, a ferry could be boarded for Victoria and Vancouver Island, with several stops along the way in the San Juan Islands, on one of which, Orcas Island, there was another CCC camp.

A small island in Cornet Bay is situated only a short distance across the water from the site of Camp Deception Pass. When Company 4786 arrived, it was inhabited by a single family, and accessible only by air or water. The solitary residents of the island commuted daily in a small seaplane, anchoring it on the lee side of the island, where it was safe from Pacific storms coming in from the Strait of Juan De Fuca. Many evenings, the enrollees watched the thrilling spectacle of the seaplane pilot flying under the Deception Pass bridge as he returned to his island home.

The island was near enough to the CCC camp that the family's radio could be heard when the weather was calm. In the still of a warm evening, enrollees listened as the sound of "Amos and Andy" and other broadcasts floated across the waterway.

Company 4786 continued the development of the park, including the construction of campgrounds, picnic shelters, trails, a boat dock, and ranger residences on the Whidbey Island side and on Fidalgo Island overlooking Bowman Bay.

Today, more than twenty stone and timber structures erected by the CCC remain in use at Deception Pass State Park, which is one of Washington's most popular parks. Rangers and their families occupy the residences, while another CCC building overlooking Bowman Bay now houses a CCC museum, established in a cooperative arrangement between the Washington State Parks and Recreation Commission and Everett Chapter #78, of the National Association of Civilian Conservation Corps Alumni.

Lillian Durbon at Camp Deception Pass and Camp Lewis and Clark

Lillian Durbon, part of the earlier "overhead" at the camp, was one of the relatively few women to work for the CCC. Earlier, she and her husband, Carroll Henry Durbon, and their three children had made their home on Orcas Island. Mr. Durbon, a forest ranger, served as foreman at CCC Camp Moran. Unfortunately, he became ill while serving there, and shortly afterward died in a

Seattle hospital on Christmas day 1935, leaving Lillian with three sons—aged seven, nine, and eleven—to raise.

Consequently, she served as the "property custodian" at Camp Deception Pass from June to November 1936, in the year before the Missourians of Company 4786 arrived. Lillian next was transferred to Camp Lewis and Clark, SP-2, twelve miles south of Chehalis, Washington, to serve that camp in the same capacity. Lewis and Clark State Park, a natural "timber museum," contains one of the very last great stands of old growth timber in the lowlands of western Washington or Oregon.

Lillian now lives on the Yakima Indian Reservation in the Yakima Valley, where she takes pride in owning pedigree bulldogs and raising quarter horses. As one of the few females hired by the 3C's organization, she has many fond memories of the CCC and its accomplishments.

Arkansas Boys at Ohanapecosh, Mt. Rainier National Park

In the summer of 1937, Mr. William S. Nowlin, a landscape architect, was directing the work of 140 Arkansas enrollees in the southeast corner of Mt. Rainier National Park. Nowlin, a middle-aged man with twenty years of professional experience, happened to be a good friend of U. S. Representative Charles H. Leavy of the state of Washington. Leavy was a strong proponent of the National Parks system and the CCC.

On June 12, Nowlin sat down to write a letter to the congressman, describing the CCC company's activities along the Ohanapecosh River. Upon receiving the letter, Leavy was so pleased by its substance that he read lengthy extracts from it in a speech before the U. S. House of Representatives in Washington, D. C., on July 8, 1937. Here are excerpts from Nowlin's informative and entertaining letter:

"All's quiet along the Ohanapecosh except the raindrops pattering on my tent. It can rain so easily here. The clouds seem to hang on the treetops and release the moisture so gently, so cheerfully, and so unceasingly. The sun is always on the point of breaking through but never quite succeeds . . .

"All week these CCC Arkansas boys have worked out in the woods uncomplainingly until yesterday. They put on those Army rainproof clothes—tin pants, they call 'em. They lean them up against a stump, climb up on top and jump into them. They are about as stiff as a suit of armor, like the knights used to wear, except the armor had joints at the knees and elbows. They do not clank or ring but when they walk it makes a noise like filing a saw.

"One of my 'gang' (A little fellow weighing about 100 pounds) came out to work the other day without his 'tin pants' and I sent him back to get them. There was only one pair left—size 44. Well, he got into them, bent the bottoms up so that he could walk, found a piece of half-inch rope, made a gallus [suspenders] to hold them up, and on the way back he gathered moss enough to fill them out around the waist and he also made himself a wig and some whiskers of moss and reported 'ready for duty.' These boys have a sense of humor.

"There is such a variety and contrast to this work. One day we are planting delicate, lacy ferns on the bank of a stream and laying a carpet of green moss around them . . . the next day we will be digging with a steam shovel or using a 'Cherry picker' to replace weathered boulders, weighing about a ton, to keep these 'dumb' campers from driving where they are not supposed to.

"Then we build huge log tables, so heavy the people can't move them around, and stone fireplaces[,] and stencil and carve and burn signs on the face of a cedar log cut in half, and build trails and footpaths, and haul gravel in dump trucks to surface roads, and, believe me, these boys are workers. They average over 20 years old, and most of this camp has had more than a year's experience in national park work (which is a lucky thing for me). The hardest task is to have work enough lined up to keep them busy. I assign them a job what I think will last all day, and in a few hours the leader will come and ask what to do next . . .

"I hope they make the C.C.C. permanent, even if they have to discontinue the Army and Navy. It's a great character-building institution. They get better training than in any school or college. I think it is the greatest thing the present administration has done.

"I wish you could see this river—the Ohanapecosh . . . On a hot day, when the glacier silt comes down, it turns milky white; when rain is falling the water is green and white, and at times it appears blue and white. It is always in such a hurry and is always singing . . .

"We have a baseball team, but we have to go 42 miles to find an open space big enough for a diamond, and a ball over the outfielder's head is lost forever in the jungles. When these boys are dressed up, ready to go to a dance or somewhere, they might be so many boys from any college in the country. They are tall, husky, and fine-looking lads and they dress nicely.

"Talk to them and [with] the first two words they speak you will know they are from the South. [In] The next 10 words it is apparent that they are either from Arkansas or Tennessee. Then ask them if they ever heard of Bob Burns and their expressions of pride will immediately eliminate Tennessee. They can tell you to an inch how far they live from Van Buren." [Vaudevillian performer Bob Burns from Van Buren, Arkansas, went on national radio in 1930, quickly becoming a celebrity for his backwoods humor and the playing of the "bazooka," a musical instrument reportedly invented by him.]

Camp Soda Springs

Two Army reserve officers, Lieutenant Merrill Pimentel and Lieutenant Robert Lueck, accompanied by twelve men, arrived at Soda Springs on the North Fork of Ahtanum Creek on June 27, 1935, to break ground for a Soil Conservation Service camp. Designated as Camp Soda Springs, SCS-6, the site was situated in rolling range and forest country about thirty-five miles west of Yakima.

The men lived in tents while they built the camp. On August 4, 1935, additional men arrived, finding that only the frames of the buildings were completed—there were no doors, windows, or lighting. The balance of Company 2942 came in on August 12, 1935. When completed by the end of the summer, Camp Soda

Springs consisted of four barracks, officers' quarters, a mess hall, a recreation hall, an administration office, two bathhouses, and a garage. Other facilities were added as the need arose.

Company 2942 was the only CCC unit to ever occupy the camp. Lieutenant Louis Cleaver, an Air Corps reservist, shaped the boys into an efficient unit. (Cleaver later resigned to fly for a commercial airline, and, in 1937, met a tragic end in a plane crash.)

When the frozen ground thawed that first spring, the members of the company shuddered to discover that the camp stood in an old riverbed. This meant that the boys would spend their Saturdays hauling in dirt to cover the stoney ground in order to plant grass on it. The boys were not able to complete this work in the summer of 1936, but had to bring in topsoil during the following year as well.

Excitement struck on a May morning when the officers' quarters burned down. The junior officer got out with only slight injuries, but all of his personal possessions, with the exception of his pajamas, were consumed by the flames.

In the summer of 1936, the enrollees cut a playing field out of the pine forest, finishing it in time to be utilized as a landing area for a wintertime ski jump.

According to an account by enrollee Jim Von Spacher, Company 2942's day began when a 6:00 A.M. bugle blare awakened the boys in their barracks beds. After that, a song was played over the public address system:

> *Put on an old pair of shoes,*
> *We'll go walking down the alley,*
> *Maybe we'll run into Sally,*
> *And the friends we used to know.*
> *Put on an old pair of shoes,*
> *We'll go walking down the alley,*
> *Maybe we'll run into Sally and Joe.*

And then came the bugle call:

You can't get 'em up,
You can't get 'em up,
You can't get 'em up in the morning!

Then someone yelled, "Grab your socks and hit the docks!" All of the young men in the barracks came alive, with pushing, shoving, and good natured horseplay on the way to the washroom. The hearty breakfast consisted of cereal, ham, bacon, eggs, pancakes, potatoes, milk, coffee, tea, cocoa, fruit, and "sidearms" (salt, pepper, sugar, etc.).

Everyone mustered at the flagpole for roll call, and they "had just better not be late." The crew trucks stood by for loading, and all the lunches were packed and ready to go (for further details about camp life, see Appendix One, the *Camp Soda Springs Behavior Book*).

Irrigation was the lifeblood of the Ahtanum Valley, and Company 2942 developed an important irrigation and water conservation system for the downstream ranches and farms. Ditches were dug to divert springs into main channels, which in turn carried water to meadows and fields. Dams were built to control erosion, and the hills of the Ahtanum watershed were surveyed for the placement of contour ditches to collect rainwater and snowmelt for agricultural use. Considerable terracing was done on the hills and ridges, and log drift fences were constructed to help control soil depletion due to overgrazing by sheep and cattle.

On the Wallace Wiley ranch, twenty collecting and distributing ditches were completed, and other irrigation systems were dug on other farms as well. Headgates likewise were constructed to control water disbursement.

A side camp was established at Green Lake, located eight miles west at the headwaters of the North Fork of Ahtanum Creek. One of the duties for the boys at the side camp was the digging of test pits to gather data for the Soil Conservation Service. Geologist S. N. Twiss, of the SCS office in Spokane, spent much time at Green Lake and Camp Soda Springs collecting information. After making many friends among the cadre and enrollees, he finished his fieldwork on July 12, 1939, just before the company was reassigned to a different locality.

Recreation always was popular at Camp Soda Springs, and in all seasons. In late 1936, the basketball team made it to the district semifinals, and, that winter, toboggans and skis were purchased with company funds to use on a nearby steep hill. The company newspaper, *The Landscaper*, reported "no serious injuries marred the snow fun."

The Landscaper, on July 25, 1939, reported that the camp's fine softball team, the "Sparks," had won many games in the Yakima Valley Softball League, including victories over the "Shurfine" and "Signal Oil" teams. Outstanding "Sparks" players included "Fields" at pitcher and first base, catcher "Dyson," shortstop "Murray," and "Coleman" at first base and also pitcher.

Camp Soda Springs stood in the wild eastern foothills of the Cascades, where wildlife was abundant. Chipmunks and ground squirrels frequented the camp, where they learned to beg for candy, nuts, and other tidbits from the boys. The small camp visitors became so tame that they ran up the arms and legs of the enrollees to reach treats offered to them. Practical jokers among the boys sometimes gave them puffed breakfast cereal, instead of their favorite snack, peanuts. The squirrels almost looked surprised as the cereal dissolved in their mouth pouches before they could run and hide it in their caches.

In August 1939, the company was ordered to abandon Soda Springs and move to Camp Waterville, near Waterville, Washington, in the high plateau wheat country of the north-central Columbia Basin. For two months, an advance crew had been setting up portable buildings and getting the camp ready to receive the full complement of men.

About twenty-five men remained at Camp Soda Springs to complete last minute details, including the dismantling of some SCS buildings. Tent platforms and other materials used at the Green Lake side camp were trucked to the Soil Conservation Service camp at Goldendale, home of Company 945, SCS-8.

Evidence of the work accomplished by the boys at Camp Soda Springs remains visible a half-century later. The log drift fences and the contour terracing, now weathered and deteriorating, of course, still can be seen in the hills and mountains surrounding the beautiful Ahtanum Valley. Some of the original Camp Soda Springs CCC buildings are utilized as part of a Forest Service work center, and the locality's camping facilities, which were developed by the enrollees, are enjoyed by hundreds of people annually.

Camp North Bend

On October 21, 1933, three Army officers from a disbanded CCC camp in Wyoming were sent by train to Bremerton, Washington, to organize a new CCC company. Accompanying them were two enlisted men. At Bremerton, they established Camp Ostrich Bay, which was completed by November 15, 1933. The new enrollees were assigned to local projects. (Later, in 1936-1937, the Missourians of Company 4786 were stationed here, as previously related in this chapter.)

Orders for moving the company to North Bend came a year and a half later. On April 24, 1935, an advance detachment was dispatched to begin work on the new camp, which was located a short distance east of the town of North Bend. On July 2, the rest of Company 2911 arrived to clear the site and construct the buildings. After much hard work, Camp North Bend, F-85, stood finished on August 14, 1935.

It was in a beautiful location along the clear, cold Snoqualmie River in the foothills of the Cascades. Later, a side camp was established up the Middle Fork of the Snoqualmie River, near potential "hot spots" during fire season (in fact, the enrollees of Company 2911 battled no less than thirty blazes by 1937, earning for themselves a reputation for their efforts).

In addition to routine forestry work and the strenuous, but exciting, work of fighting fires, Camp North Bend was called upon to help out in uncommon emergency situations, arising from the fact that the company was stationed along the main east-west travel and recreational corridor through the Cascades. Just two days after the full complement of men arrived, word came that a girl was lost on Mt. Si, a high, rugged, heavily timbered peak just north of North Bend. On July 4, 1935, one quarter of the company's enrollees scoured Mt. Si for the missing girl. On the morning of July 5, after twenty-four hours of searching, she was found alive and brought down from the mountain. Though the rescue effort was lengthy, difficult, and strenuous, the boys were pleased to have been of assistance in a life threatening emergency.

On February 22, 1936, the camp received a call for men and equipment to help clear snow from the Snoqualmie Pass highway. Most of the boys participated in the effort, removing snow and assisting traffic along the icy roadway. In May of the same year, a report came that an airplane had crashed among the close-by peaks. A sizeable search party set out seeking the downed aircraft. They found the debris, and "with great difficulty" managed to haul out the victims, who had perished in the crash.

After work hours, of course, the enrollees were free to pursue their own choice of activities, whether it be hobbies, movies, sports, educational courses, or, perhaps, just lounging around. Some boys tried their hand at panning for gold in the Snoqualmie River flowing past the camp. In periods of extreme fire danger, however, very little time was available to pursue individual interests.

At times, the mess officer was hard pressed to feed the men complete, well balanced meals on twenty-eight cents a day per man, even with the low cost of food in the lean depression years. This probably accounted for "slumgullion" on the menu. The ingredients in this famous (or infamous!) concoction varied from cook to cook, and from camp to camp. Subsequently, the palatability of the different types of "slumgullion" varied also. It seemed to be served occasionally in all of the camp mess halls.

But, as one enrollee stated, "Any food is better than no food at all, even 'slumgullion,' and at home that is what I had—'no food!'"

The "slumgullion" referred to was a "cross between a watery stew and hash, made of leftovers from the day before."

According to a veteran of Camp North Bend, "The food got so bad one time when we were fighting a forest fire that the crew refused to go back on the fire line until better food was served. The food situation was well taken care of by the company commander, however, and we did not have that problem again while I was stationed there."

One veteran later recalled being served mashed potato sandwiches (i. e., mashed potatoes between two slices of bread). He believed Camp North Bend literally served the worst chow in the CCC.

Today, the old 3C's facility is owned by Seattle's Highline School District, and has been renamed Camp Waskowitz for a former University of Washington football player and World War II hero. Except for the addition of a swimming pool, the camp remains little altered, appearing much as it did when occupied by Company 2911 in the 1930s. In fact, it may well be the best preserved of any CCC camp remaining in the Pacific Northwest.

The facility is used year around by students and other groups for outings, classwork, social gatherings, and outdoor instruction. Also, each September, as many as three hundred members of the National Association of Civilian Conservation Corps Alumni meet here, exchanging fond memories of the years they served in the CCC for five dollars a month "pocket money." Many Camp North Bend veterans remain in the Pacific Northwest. They return often, recounting tales about the "good old days in the CCC," the "slumgullion," and the chipped beef on toast (known by a different name in the CCC).

Camp Moran

This camp stood in Moran State Park, on beautiful Orcas Island in San Juan County. The property had been given to the state in the 1920s by Robert Moran, a ship builder and former mayor of Seattle (Moran was mayor when the great 1889 fire destroyed downtown Seattle).

Few improvements had been made to Moran State Park prior to the arrival of Company 1233 in the spring of 1933. The boys from New York and New Jersey found the "barest" of camp facilities and no electricity. In fact, at the time, there were only a few small villages and some scattered residences on the large island.

Company 1233 quickly set up "skeleton" facilities, consisting of Army tents, with kitchen, mess hall, and dispensary. The camp stood in a picturesque setting near Cascade Lake, just inside the park boundary. As soon as they were situated in their new "home," they started work on park improvements.

Preceding their arrival, Carroll Durbon had been assigned to assist in selecting a site for the camp. Durbon, a forest ranger, served as a senior foreman for State Parks. Once the "Eastern boys" were settled in, Durbon supervised park improvements, and he also trained the enrollees for fire fighting and fire suppression work on Orcas and other islands in the San Juans. The building of a permanent camp was planned for later, as work in the park progressed.

It was springtime—the weather was mild and sunny, and strawberries were ripe for harvesting. Lillian, the wife of the senior foreman, arrived on the island with the CCC boys. She and several other park employee wives picked strawberries, and baked pies for their families and the lads in camp. The fresh pie was a welcome treat for the "city boys," so far from home.

The enrollees quickly adjusted, of course, learning to work and live in harmony with their comrades in a healthy outdoor environment. They enjoyed the fresh air and mild climate of the region, as well as the unspoiled beauty of Orcas Island, with its lakes, mountains, forests, and beaches. They hiked, combed the shoreline, fished in the lakes and sound, and gathered oysters and clams.

Wildlife abounded, and, in off duty hours, the boys often sat on the beaches watching migrating whales offshore. As many as a hundred were counted in a few hours, as one fascinated whale watching enrollee later recollected. Deer and especially rabbits were plentiful, and there were no dangerous or poisonous animals or plants on the island. The prolific rabbits were the offspring from a rabbit farm that had been abandoned by the owner, leaving the bunnies free to run wild and multiply.

State Parks planned many projects to keep the boys busy, but the major accomplishment was the rebuilding of the road up Mt. Constitution and the construction of a beautiful stone tower atop the peak. Years earlier, roadways had been cleared to the summit, but, being little more than trails winding along the slopes, they were largely inadequate for vehicular traffic.

The enrollees blasted out boulders to widen and improve the route, while setting aside stones to be used in constructing the tower on top of the 2,409 feet high mountain. They graded and surfaced the road, sloped the banks, "daylighted" curves, and constructed log guardrails, which were much appreciated by motorists driving the steep roadway. As the road was completed, work began on the Mt. Constitution tower.

Meanwhile, twenty-five enrollees were sent to a side camp at the University of Washington's oceanographic research center on San Juan Island. The camp officially opened on a Saturday, October 19, 1935, and soon gained a reputation as one of the best CCC facilities in the entire Fort Lewis District. Friday Harbor residents and others on the island welcomed the boys, making their stay a pleasant and unforgettable one.

A new complement of men occupied Camp Moran, SP-1, in October 1936, when Company 4768 from Minnesota replaced the "East Coast" lads, who were transferred elsewhere. Company 4768 was new, assembled only about a week before at Fort Snelling. On October 12, 1936, at 9:30 in the evening, they had entrained for the long trip westward across the plains and mountains to Anacortes. It was only then, during the long trip, that they learned their destination was Olga on Orcas Island in Puget Sound.

At Camp Moran, they found "only the barest skeleton of a camp." Within a year, however, Captain William Baily was able to buy and acquire equipment worth about $2,500 (in depression era prices, of course), upgrading the camp into one of the best outfitted CCC facilities in the Pacific Northwest. Among other items, Baily brought in two washing machines, kitchen equipment, a complete set of power and hand tools for the woodworking shop (including a lathe, planner, rip saw, and jig saw), office equipment (notably five typewriters and two adding machines), a fully equipped darkroom for photographic purposes, a movie projector, two pool tables, four sets of "overstuffed" furniture for the library, and a great amount of athletic equipment. Company 4768 also acquired "its own navy"—a forty feet long officers' launch formerly used by the crew of the aircraft carrier *Saratoga*.

The new company soon constructed nine miles of fire-breaks and five miles of truck trails, but, largely due to the fire prevention lecturing and training by superintendent L. H. Anderson and other foremen, no fires broke out in the park in late 1936 and 1937. Other accomplishments in the park included the completion of a cement reservoir, a boathouse and woodshed enclosed within a log palisade, a pair of outdoor kitchens, a topographical survey of State Parks property, hiking trails, ranger residences, and log shelters. Some "new boys" from Arkansas and Missouri arrived to fill company vacancies in 1937.

The most impressive project, of course, was the erection of the tower atop Mt. Constitution. It was designed by famed Seattle architect Ellsworth Storey who spent six years here supervising 3C's work. The handsome stone structure's design reportedly was patterned after centuries old watchtowers in Europe's Caucasus Mountains. Sandstone used in its construction came from quarries at the north end of Orcas Island and on nearby Sucia Island, and from the slopes of Mt. Constitution where the crews rebuilt the roadway. Using hand tools, enrollees cut and sized the stones, fitting them into place.

After its completion, the tower served as a tourist attraction and as a fire lookout, and also was a coastal observation post during World War II. It stands on the highest point in the San Juan Islands, commanding a spectacular view of the Olympic Peninsula, the Strait of Juan De Fuca, Puget Sound, the Canadian gulf islands, Vancouver Island, the snow crowned Cascade Range, and numerous cities and towns in both British Columbia and Washington.

As at so many CCC camps, Company 4768 organized competitive baseball and basketball teams. In 1937, Gilbert Schaefer, the star pitcher and captain of the baseball team, was designated a "CCC All-American" by *Happy Days*.

The lads were welcome in nearby communities, where they attended dances and other community gatherings, and visited individual households. The ever active Captain Baily arranged for free ferry transportation to and from the mainland, low rates at hotels and restaurants, and inexpensive fares for movies in Eastsound, Friday Harbor, Anacortes, and Bellingham (just ten cents at theaters in the latter three towns). In return, Camp Moran hosted Governor Clarence Martin, community Chamber of Commerce organizations, and teachers and school groups, as well as an annual "grand open-house."

Educational opportunities were wide-ranging, including "Aeronautics, auto mechanics, blue print reading, forestry, radio, photography, arithmetic, English, geography, history, cooking and baking, first-aid, health, leadership training, social ethics, current events, and many others." Several boys attended Orcas Island High School.

Camp Tieton

On October 10, 1936, Company 4769 was formed at Fort Snelling, Minnesota, and two days later entrained for the state of Washington. Upon arriving in Yakima on October 14, trucks picked up the enrollees at the station, convoying them thirty-eight miles up the Naches and Tieton rivers to Camp Tieton, F-28. Meanwhile, Company 1650, which had occupied the camp, had returned to Illinois. The roster of Company 4769, consisting of 148 Minnesotians and several local LEM's, was added to until Camp Tieton's manpower neared 175 men. Much work was done in the following months, with the most impressive being the construction of a ninety feet long steel bridge in the Clear Creek vicinity of the North Fork of the Tieton River, located a few miles east of White Pass. Work at the camp itself included the construction of new buildings and a barn, renovating other facilities, and constructing a residence for Arnold Arneson, the Tieton District Ranger.

By late 1937, the Minnesota boys also had completed eleven miles of new road, while improving other existing roadway, and strung up more than twenty miles of telephone lines, despite interruptions due to snowy weather or fire fighting. A "spike" camp stood sixteen miles southwest on Pinegrass Ridge (south of today's Rimrock Lake), enabling the boys to cut roads and fire trails far back into the mountains.

In 1937, fifty enrollees were dispatched to the big "Spud Hill" fire. Also, in September of that year, another sixty-six men were sent to fight the Skykomish blaze in the Stevens Pass vicinity. They helped squelch other fires as well.

On October 13, 1937, a hundred "junior" enrollees from Missouri arrived, and, a week later, seventeen more came, replacing those men who had completed their enlistments or were discharged for other reasons. Company strength now was 200, and the boys cut a thousand cords of wood for the camp's wintertime use.

Typically, there were frequent changes in the company's "overhead," as foremen, LEM's, Army officers, etc. were brought in or transferred elsewhere. Most unusual, though, was the large number of doctors that came and went at Camp Tieton. In a year's span, from late 1936 to late 1937, no less than ten physicians succeeded each other as the camp doctor.

CCC-Indian Division, at Fort Simcoe State Park and Signal Peak

The Civilian Conservation Corps also recruited Indians to partici-pate in soil conservation and forestry projects on the Colville, Spokane, Warm Springs, and other Indian reservations in the Pacific Northwest (other Native Americans across the nation were enlisted to work on their own reservations as well). Normally, after a day's work, Indian enrollees returned to their homes for the evening, but some Indian companies did reside full time in barracks.

The main camp on the Yakima Indian Reservation stood at historic Fort Simcoe, situated twenty-seven miles west of Top-penish. Established in 1856, Fort Simcoe was occupied by the U. S. Army until 1859, after which time it was an Indian agency for many years. Today, this outstanding example of an early territorial military post is administered by the Washington State Parks and Recreation Commission.

Yakima CCC enrollees also served in a primary summer camp at Signal Peak, located in the heart of the reservation backcountry near Mt. Adams. Other side camps were scattered throughout the reservation's forest lands as needed for specific projects or fire protection. The Forestry Department of the Bureau of Indian Affairs, which administered the Signal Peak Ranger District, directed the CCC recruits.

The BIA's foresters decided to maintain winter quarters in the forest to combat pine beetle infestations. Three man teams, consisting of a pair of cruisers and a compass man, identified infected trees and marked them on topographical maps. "Bug crews," using these maps, went out to cut down and burn the trees, which could be safely done in winter or the wetter months of the year.

One spring day in 1934, cruisers found a pair of bear cubs and brought them back to the Signal Peak Ranger Station. According to enrollee Orville Olney, who was assigned there at the time, the cubs were bawling from hunger when they arrived in camp. Because the camp was snowed in, no one could get to town (White Swan) for baby nipples to be used in feeding the infant bears. Relying on their ingenuity, the enrollees used catsup bottles stuffed with old socks in the necks to control the flow of milk.

Named Suzie and Cactus by the Indian enrollees, the bears became voracious eaters, and, when weaned, often fought over their food. When free, they raided the camp looking for tasty morsels. At night, they remained tied to the base of a small fir tree. Suzie climbed the tree one evening, and, unfortunately, managed to hang herself.

Cactus survived for a time, faring well. When the call was sounded at mealtime, he headed for the mess hall intending to "chow down" with all of the other guys! The cook kept him out with a broom.

Sometimes, Cactus stationed himself by the main office, checking out vehicles coming into camp. He scared more than one visitor, who suddenly found himself "eyeball to eyeball" with a bear!

According to Olney, "We had a heavy snowpack of five feet or so. We lived in pyramid tents and had paths shoveled to all the facilities. About every two weeks, Cactus would awaken from hibernation and roam about, visiting everyone in camp, then return to his winter headquarters behind the potbellied stove in the toolroom of the warehouse, where the cruisers turned in their equipment every evening. There, Cactus could watch it all."

When the mountain roads opened up in the spring, the married men were allowed to have their families move into the camp. Children played with Cactus, feeding him tasty morsels as he stood on his hind legs begging to be fed. One mother, seeing her young child face to face with the bear, screamed. Cactus bounded away in fright, bowling over a couple of children. Regrettably, this episode cost him his freedom and happiness.

He was crated off to the Spokane zoo, away from his CCC companions. He never ceased crying and whimpering, refused all food and water, and, according to the zoo officials, died of a broken heart.

Olney served four years in the CCC, followed by twenty years in the U. S. Marine Corps. Returning to Toppenish, he worked as Chief of Police and then Chief Judge on the tribal court of the Yakima Indian Nation, retiring after twenty years of service in law enforcement and the courtroom.

The Tillamook Burn of Northwest Oregon

On August 14, 1933, one of the most destructive forest fires in recent Pacific Northwest history broke out in the coastal mountains west of Portland. Starting near Tillamook, the flames crowned in the tops of 200 feet tall trees, and, fanned by the wind and the fire's own updrafts, the roaring conflagration rapidly advanced on a fifteen mile front.

As flames leaped from tree crown to tree crown, hurricane-like winds uprooted and toppled 400 year old Douglas fir trees. Thick, blinding smoke settled in the valleys, blotting out the sun.

In twenty-four hours, the blaze consumed 240,000 acres, destroying timber and wildlife, and ruining watersheds.

One thousand CCC "tree troopers" were rushed from the camps to the inferno, joining two thousand other fire fighters from the region. Fire fighting had to be done by hand. Access was difficult; there were few roads in the rugged coastal mountains.

The CCC, which was a brand new organization at the time, proved itself in the fierce struggle. Trained for the task, they performed like veterans, working long hours in the heat, smoke, and hot cinders. Tragedy struck, however, when one enrollee, Frank Palmer of Illinois, was killed by a falling tree. Before it was brought under control, the fire devastated 311,000 acres.

After the flames were extinguished, hundreds of enrollees worked in the cleanup. From Camp Nehalem, P-221, close to the coast, Camp Rehers, P-227, near the Wilson River summit, and Camp Trask, P-217, fifteen miles east of Tillamook, the CCC planted trees, revamped and intensified fire suppression work in the area, and developed recreational facilities.

They built trails, roads, lookout towers, bridges, campgrounds, and picnic areas. A permanent fire dispatch network was instituted, and a number of firehall headquarters were established. These were major steps in creating a permanent fire control organization. In off duty hours on weekends and holidays—except during periods of extreme fire danger, of course—the CCC lads traveled to Seaside and other nearby resort towns to enjoy the beaches, roller skating, and other activities.

Six years later, in 1939, another fire swept across 190,000 acres of the coastal range, much of it in the original burned over area. Due to the improved fire suppression program and the presence of the CCC camps, trained men were quickly brought to the fire line. In 1945, another blaze blackened 180,000 acres. Again, much of it was within the original burn. By this time, of course, the CCC had been disbanded, but the improvements they had made in the region proved invaluable in the fire fighting effort.

The three fires collectively known as the Tillamook burn blackened 350,000 acres (almost 550 square miles) of timberland. An estimated 13.1 billion board feet of prime lumber was lost.

Today, forests have regrown in the Tillamook burn and abound with wildlife. Many of the CCC-built roads, trails, bridges, lookouts, campgrounds, and picnic facilities yet remain, and are visible reminders of the historic role of the CCC in the region during the 1930s and early 1940s.

Mt. Hood: Timberline Lodge and Camp Zig Zag

Company 928 was assembled at Vancouver Barracks less than two months after the creation of the CCC by the U. S. Congress in March 1933. By May 14, a site at Zig Zag, Oregon, near Mt. Hood, was selected, and construction began on what would turn out to be the oldest continuously occupied camp in the Vancouver Barracks District.

Eleven days later, the 200 men of Company 928, who had been living in tents while constructing the camp, moved into new barracks. Shortly, the men of Camp Zig Zag, F-11, began working on Forest Service projects, constructing roads, trails, bridges, telephone lines, and campgrounds, as well as doing patrol duty, fire fighting, reforestation, and general cleaning up. A Zig Zag sawmill operated by the enrollees cut the massive cedar timbers used in constructing the rugged picnic tables in the camp-grounds. The most impressive project, however, was the erection of Timberline Lodge on the southern slopes of Mt. Hood beginning in 1935.

Men of the Works Progress Administration and the U. S. Forest Service, with assistance from the CCC boys, constructed the large, handsome stone and wood structure. Its massive timbers were cut in the forests of the Cascade Range. The great, hexagonal, stone fireplace, the beautiful, pegged oak floors, and the large exposed beams of the lobby remain today as testimonials to the diverse and impressive skills of the WPA and CCC craftsmen.

The carved newel-posts of the stairway were cut from discarded power poles, and the andirons in the lobby's huge fireplace were handwrought from old railroad tracks. Other artwork included elaborate wood carvings, painted murals, intricate mosaics of wood and stone, and handwoven rugs made from scraps of old CCC uniforms. In addition to helping the WPA men construct the lodge, CCC enrollees also built a water system for it as well as roadway access.

On September 28, 1937, President Roosevelt, accompanied by his wife, Eleanor, dedicated Timberline Lodge. FDR's speech from the balcony on the lodge's south side was broadcast across the nation. Perched high on the mountain's shoulder at 6,000 feet elevation, the world famous lodge today remains as the pride of Oregon's best known winter sports area.

Other work accomplished at Mt. Hood by the lads from Camp Zig Zag included the cutting of a ten mile long bridle path between Government Camp and Rhododendron. Also, improvements were made to the ski bowl and ski trails, such as the building of a warming hut with a large fireplace, and the construction of a judge's stand at the ski jump.

Crews also built 37.6 mile long Timberline Trail, encircling Mt. Hood, mostly between an elevation of 5,000 to 6,000 feet. Enrollees erected stone shelters at intervals along the route. Today, some of these rustic structures are in ruins, but others still remain intact and are utilized by hikers on this exceedingly popular trail.

CCC Director Robert Fechner on an inspection tour of Camp Columbia, Grand Coulee, Washington. Previously a noted labor leader, Fechner guided the 3C's from its inception in 1933 until his death on December 31, 1939. He was succeeded by James McEntee. *Manuscripts, Archives, and Special Collections, Washington State University Library, Pullman*

Chapter Eight

ACCOMPLISHMENTS ACROSS THE USA

As I look back over the actual measures which were undertaken in this first year [of FDR's presidency], *I realize that the one in which my husband took the greatest pleasure was the establishment on April 5, 1933, of the Civilian Conservation Corps camps.*

Eleanor Roosevelt

I n less than a decade, the Civilian Conservation Corps changed the face of much of America. There really is no way to fully evaluate and acknowledge all of the benefits resulting from the gigantic program carried out by the CCC, either of its impact on our national landscape, or its molding of the character and bodies of 3,000,000 Americans. Most of these enrollees, of course, were youths, but 225,000 of them were World War I veterans, who, organized into their own companies, were given a chance to rebuild their lives in the camps.

The total list of projects undertaken and completed by the CCC would fill several books. This legacy is clearly evident in every state of the Union—the parks and campgrounds, dams and lakes, regenerated forests and farmland, wildlife refuges and wilderness areas, historic sites, lookout towers, trails, roads, and bridges. In addition, millions of acres of land were mapped and surveyed by enrollees.

The rustic, but handsome, CCC buildings, constructed of logs, stone, and other handcrafted materials, are especially noteworthy for compatibility with their surrounding environment, whether it be in a park, National Forest, or wildlife refuge. An awareness is growing today that these structures are an important part of our cultural heritage. Steps now are being taken by federal and state agencies to protect and preserve the best of them for future generations.

The CCC and National Defense, 1940-1942

The CCC probably did as much to prepare the United States for participation in World War II as any other government agency, not excluding the U. S. military. Ninety percent of the 3,000,000 CCC enrollees later served their country in wartime. They were accustomed to barracks life and knew how to get along with others. And, they were disciplined, having learned not only how to take orders, but also how to give them. Approximately 50,000 reserve officers also gained valuable experience in the CCC, leading and administering men at the company level or at district headquarters.

With their "let's get it done" attitude, CCC veterans worked well together—except, of course, for some "goldbricks" afflicted with "under achievementitis," which can be found in any large organization. Overall, the CCC training and spirit were vital when the United States entered the war following the December 7, 1941, Japanese attack on Pearl Harbor, Hawaii.

In the last year of peace, eighty CCC camps across the nation were established at Army, Navy, and Marine installations under the supervision of the War Department. Enrollees helped construct barracks, airfields, target ranges, parachute landing sites, off-post recreational centers, and other facilities. The boys also did the type of work for which the CCC was famous—building firebreaks, roads, trails, and telephone and water systems on military reservations. At military hospitals and reception centers, CCC enrollees served as clerks, bookkeepers, cooks, bakers, grounds keepers, and maintenance personnel.

The CCC education and training program also was expanded by September 1940 with national defense goals in mind. An emphasis was placed on developing those noncombatant skills that were essential to the functioning of a modern military organization. In 1941, 266,759 enrollees completed units of vocational instruction. In a typical instance, five-hundred enrollees were assigned to work alongside skilled mechanics at fifty-five motor repair shops. Over 1,000 enrollees also were being trained, at any one time, at forty-four cooking and baking schools, in courses ranging in length from several weeks to two months. Thousands of CCC-trained cooks and bakers later served in the mess halls of the Army, Navy, and Marine Corps, as did the CCC-trained auto mechanics at military motor pools in the United States and overseas.

In 1941, five-hundred enrollees at a time were attending twenty-six radio schools, learning to become radio operators and technicians. These men were in great demand, of course, not only in the CCC and the military services, but also in private industry.

CCC Requiem, July 30, 1942

By the time that the United States entered the war, thousands of enrollees already had left the CCC to enlist in the armed forces or take work in defense industries. The unemployment problems of the previous decade vanished as the military services, factories, railroads, and farms began making ever greater demands on the nation's manpower.

Furthermore, due to the upswing in the wartime economy and improvements in the efforts of government agencies to meet social and welfare needs, most families at home no longer needed their sons' CCC pay to get by. In fact, by 1937 the "relief" provision for new recruits had been removed; young men from more financially secure families were allowed to enroll. Thus, the CCC's primary function as a welfare agency had become outmoded.

The exodus of enrollees from the CCC continued at a rapid rate, while at the same time there was an increasing shortage of eligible new recruits. In wartime, the nation's young men simply were needed elsewhere.

Thus, after nine years of outstanding service, the end of the always popular CCC was at hand. With deep regret, the U.S. House and Senate terminated the Civilian Conservation Corps on July 30, 1942. The House voted $8,000,000 for its dissolution, paying for the process of turning over the CCC's organizational structure, facilities, and equipment to the War Department and other agencies.

The Legacy

In 1941, a study prepared for Congress disclosed that the future physical value of the work completed by the CCC exceeded $1,750,000,000. "Roosevelt's Tree Army" had reversed the traditional pattern of using up or wasting the nation's natural resources at a faster rate than they were being replenished. Approximately 200 major kinds of conservation work had been undertaken on forest, agricultural, park, and other lands.

The following table, adapted from the Federal Security Agency's annual report for 1941, indicates the great magnitude of work accomplished by the CCC from April 5, 1933, through 1941:

> 38,087 vehicular bridges
> 26,368,296 rods of fencing
> 83,548 miles of new telephone lines
> 23,725 new water sources
> 122,169 miles of truck trails and minor roads
> 5,875,578 erosion check dams

2,246,100,600 trees planted
3,998,328 acres of forest stand improvement
6,304,211 man days fighting forest fires
6,192,269 man days of fire presuppression and prevention
20,934,581 acres of tree and plant disease and pest control
operations . . .

In addition, the 4,500 "main" camps across the nation and in Alaska, Hawaii, Puerto Rico, and the Virgin Islands, built more than 3,000 lookout towers, over 8,000 foot and pack bridges, thousands of buildings and structures, and hundreds of state parks.

In the 1930s, the 3C's boys played a major role in controlling the "Dust Bowl" of the nation's central region. Crop withering drought and gigantic dust storms, darkening the midday sun, forced tens of thousands of families into bankruptcy and abandonment of their farms. Those farmers that did remain were just barely hanging on. In a massive effort, CCC boys planted windbreaks, or shelterbreaks, strategically scattered across the Great Plains from Canada to Mexico. The shelterbreaks— 233,000,000 trees in all—helped stop severe erosion, and aided in the protection of wildlife as well as agricultural land.

Everywhere in America, the CCC provided assistance during emergencies, saving lives and property when natural disasters struck. Enrollees were ready and eager to help wherever floods, fires, hurricanes, or snowstorms threatened communities. Also, on numerous occasions, they searched for downed planes or missing persons in mountains, deserts, or forest.

In 1937 near Madisonville, Kentucky, CCC boys moved out over 200 families, as well as their livestock and other possessions, from houses and farms flooded by the Pond and Green rivers. When Gainesville, Georgia, was devastated by a cyclone in the early 1930s, enrollees from Robertstown and other camps guarded against pillaging. My brother, Clayton, was one of these boys. He noted that the tornado had carried a large bell all the way across town.

Throughout America, the CCC also saved and protected historic sites of local, regional, and national significance—nearly 4,000 all together. In one instance, a former CCC camp even became one of our nation's most important historic places. This occurred when FDR selected a former CCC camp on a Maryland mountaintop as the location for a new presidential retreat, called "Shangri-La." It later was renamed "Camp David" by President Dwight Eisenhower, in honor of his grandson, David Eisenhower. Since the completion of the presidential retreat, each of our nation's "First Families" has stayed there, and, of course, numerous meetings and decisions of national and international importance have occurred within its confines.

CCC boys restored important battlefield sites, such as the Peace Memorial at Gettysburg, Pennsylvania (where General Meade's Union troops stopped General Lee and the Army of Virginia's last invasion of the North), Fort Necessity, Pennsylvania (young George Washington met defeat here at the start of the French and Indian War), Fort Pulaski, Georgia (captured in a Union Army/Navy operation in 1862), and the Andersonville National Historical Site and Cemetery, Georgia (site of the Confederacy's notorious prisoner of war camp for Union captives).

The CCC reportedly "fired the last shot" at Gettysburg in 1934! While restoring the battlefield, enrollees dug up an armed Civil War shell. The company commander thought it too dangerous to send off to a museum, so he had it exploded, with all due ceremony—the last shot fired at Gettysburg!

Enrollees reconstructed the cabin in New Salem, Illinois, where young Abraham Lincoln studied and read by the flickering light of a fireplace. The village, Lincoln's home for six years when he was a young man, was restored to its original appearance by the CCC.

The CCC developed recreational facilities in our most famous national parks and other scenic areas, from Mt. Rushmore to Death Valley, and Mammoth Cave to Mesa Verde, to name just a few. They constructed shelters along the Appalachian Trail in the Great Smoky Mountains and Shenandoah national parks. The

Blue Ridge Parkway in Virginia and North Carolina, and recreational facilities at Hoover Dam's Lake Mead National Recreational Area, were completed by enrollees from camps in those localities. Near Denver, they constructed the Red Rocks natural amphitheater, a 10,000 seat acoustical wonder where outdoor concerts, plays, and opera are performed, and they completed the preliminary work on the scenic highway along the Palisades of the Hudson River.

The CCC's "Arkansas float camp" was unusual. Here, enrollees working for the fish and wildlife service lived on a fleet of houseboats, while developing the streams, swamps, and bayous into waterfowl refuges. The boys were granted "shore leave" on weekends and holidays.

Nearly a score of CCC camps worked on the gigantic Tennessee Valley Authority dam projects. The companies were under the administrative control of the U. S. Forest Service, but the TVA directed the jobs. Enrollees operated two large tree nurseries, while working on reforestation and forest improvement, erosion control, and fisheries and wildlife management on TVA controlled lands and waterways. In 1940 alone, the boys planted 13,000,000 trees on 1,043 different soil control projects on 9,000 acres of eroded private lands.

Washington's Grand Coulee Dam, one of the great showpieces for Roosevelt's New Deal, was the largest concrete structure in the world when completed in 1941. Enrollees from Camp Columbia were there, building parks and subsidiary structures along the Columbia River, including an attractive rock wall in the town's city park (which recently was restored to its original elegance). Other CCC companies constructed most of the facilities remaining today in eleven Washington State Parks, including such attractive structures as the mountaintop Vista House in Mt. Spokane State Park, and the wood and stone footbridge across the Chehalis River at Rainbow Falls State Park.

*The National Association of Civilian Conservation Corps
Alumni; and Some Famous CCC Veterans*

In the post-war era, of course, CCC veterans entered a wide range of careers, from politics to entertainment, from education to medicine, to a host of other fields. Raymond Burr, the noted TV and movie star, served in the 3C's, as did actor Robert Mitchum. Burr, in particular, has been involved in CCC veterans' activities in recent decades. One New York enrollee recalls seeing singer Frank Sinatra as a recruit at Camp Dix, New Jersey. Sinatra, whose career took off a short while later, "had a mandolin and sang Italian songs" in the barracks.

Some veterans who have made their mark in politics include New Hampshire Governor Hugh Gallen, Virginia Congressman Dan Daniel, Minnesota Congressman John Blatnik, and Jack W. King, Chief Justice of the New Hampshire Supreme Court. State Senator Avery Garrett of Washington was a member of Company 1443, Camp Mill City, Oregon, P-214. Garrett served twenty years in the State House of Representatives, and also was mayor of Renton, Washington.

Brigadier General Leland W. Smith (now retired) of the United States Marine Corps stated: "I must give the CCC's and the U. S. Marine Corps credit for making a man out of me and giving me a start in life . . . And, all of this from a humble beginning as a CCC enrollee!"

In 1977, a group of CCC veterans formed a nonprofit organization called the National Association of Civilian Conservation Corps Alumni (NACCCA), which incorporated in California. Today, there are chapters in every state and 20,000 members, with permanent headquarters and a museum at Jefferson Barracks Historical Park, near St. Louis, Missouri. Every two years, the NACCCA has a national convention. Elsewhere across the nation, CCC alumni also gather for regional, state, and, especially, chapter reunions.

The NACCCA and its numerous chapters are dedicated to commemorating the good that the 3C's accomplished, and have encouraged the establishment of modern CCC type work organizations in several states. In 1983, the NACCCA promoted the release by the U. S. Postal Service of a first-class stamp commemorating the fiftieth anniversary of FDR's founding of the CCC. (The stamp features three enrollees in blue denim dungarees building a road.) Members of the NACCCA also have identified numerous 3C's structures, and have erected monuments in recognition of CCC deeds.

Company 290, P-233, at Shafer Butte spike camp, north of Boise, Idaho.
*Manuscripts, Archives, and Special Collections, Washington State University
Library, Pullman*

A typical CCC "tent city"—Camp Shafer Butte. *Manuscripts, Archives, and Special Collections, Washington State University Library, Pullman*

Trout Creek hydroelectric project under construction near the Wind River Experiment Station by Company 944, Camp Hemlock, in 1935. The dam is located north of Carson in Washington's Columbia River Gorge country. *Gifford Pinchot National Forest*

Don Brown operating a "35 Cletrac" bulldozer out of the Quartz Mountain side camp, summer 1936. Brown and other enrollees from Camp Taneum built a ten mile road to the Quartz Mountain lookout tower, located on the divide between the Yakima and Naches rivers. *Donald Brown*

Tower on Mt. Constitution in the San Juan Islands, hand constructed by enrollees from Camp Moran, SP-1, in the mid 1930s. *Edwin G. Hill*

Camp Darrington in Washington's north Cascades; Whitehorse peak in the distance. *Manuscripts, Archives, and Special Collections, Washington State University Library, Pullman*

"Builders of American River Ski Lodge"—Company 932, Camp Naches, F-70, November 13, 1935. Front, left to right: Stan Reynolds, Rex Dozier, *Kenneth Sprague, "Popovich," Paul Halloway, Harold Nissely. Second row:_____, _____, Pap Mortimer, Oliver Klingensmith (supt.), _____, Joe Reidinger, Harry Jewsberry. Third row: George Gasper, Paul Connor, Ernie Tate. Fourth row: Louis Garn, Darryl George, Joe Dietz, _____, Gregory Doyal. In 1984, *Ken Sprague and other CCC veterans returned to reroof this structure. *Edwin G. Hill*

Enrollees Audley "A. G." StJohn (left) and William C. West (center) with NPS Superintendent James R. McDonaghie near Farmington, Pennsylvania, July 4, 1937. *A. G. StJohn*

A. G. StJohn, with Company 5481, stopping at Paradise, Montana, while en route from Somerset, Pennsylvania, to Camp Sunset, Washington, in October 1937. *A. G. StJohn*

Dedication of the "Spirit of the CCC" statue, Balboa Park, San Diego, California, by CCC Assistant Director James McEntee and Captain Arthur Davidson, commander of Camp Ideal, May 19, 1936. Dubbed "Iron Mike" by enrollees, the statue later was moved and now is missing. *Marion Wilbur, "Spirit of the CCC" San Diego Chapter #55, NACCCA*

CCC Soil Conservation Service project. *Edwin G. Hill*

Tent camp established only weeks after FDR created the Civilian Conservation Corps; Company 603, north of Tyee Springs in the old Columbia National Forest, June 29, 1933. *Gifford Pinchot National Forest*

Company 603, June 29, 1933; Army mess kits were commonly used in the early days of the CCC. *Gifford Pinchot National Forest*

CCC bridge builders near Redfish Lake in Idaho's Sawtooth Range. *Manuscripts, Archives, and Special Collections, Washington State University Library, Pullman*

A typical erosion control dam constructed by enrollees in localities east of the Cascades. *Robert W. Larse*

Company office at CCC Camp Electron, in Pierce County, east of Tacoma, Washington, July 23, 1937. *Manuscripts, Archives, and Special Collections, Washington State University Library, Pullman*

Chapter Nine

WHERE HAVE THE CCC BOYS GONE?

Fading light dims the sight,
And a star gems the sky,
Gleaming bright.
From afar drawing nigh,
Fall the night . . .

"Taps," Fort Lewis CCC songbook, 1934

H ere are more accounts from CCC veterans, describing their days in the camps, and, in some cases, their lives afterward. Skills learned in the CCC, along with the "We can take it" attitude, helped make CCC boys into effective soldiers and sailors during World War II, and responsible and productive citizens afterward.

Obviously, slogans such as "We can take it" were common during the New Deal era. Here it might be worth noting that in the early days of the 3C's, Ray Hoyt, editor of *Happy Days*, wrote a book titled, *"We Can Take It": A Short Story of the CCC*. The 128 page booklet sold for twenty-five cents to CCC enrollees.

Donald Brown at Camp Taneum

Between April 1936 and May 1939, Donald Brown served in three CCC camps at Taneum, Quilcene, and Naches, all in the state of Washington. Today, Don is enjoying retirement at his home in Richland, Washington. Along with his other activities, he has been president of, and remains busy in, Tri-Cities Chapter #48, of the National Association of Civilian Conservation Corps Alumni:

"In my first enlistment from April 1 to October 15, 1936, I was assigned to Camp Taneum, which was under the supervision of the U. S. Forest Service during the day and directed by U. S. Army personnel at night. Camp Taneum was located in the Kittitas Valley in the Cle Elum/Ellensburg vicinity, nine miles from Thorp.

"That spring, before the upper country of the east central Cascades was dry enough to get into, we widened the road to Thorp. Luckily for me, they had just started a double shift to get the road done sooner, so I was assigned to a '35 Cletrac' bulldozer.

"I joined the camp baseball team, which played town teams on Sundays and high school teams during the week, and we did fairly well. I had to quit as of June 1, however, when all of the dump truck and bulldozer drivers were moved southwest into the Cascade foothills to a side camp of about forty men.

"Our job was to extend a road about ten miles to the Quartz Mountain lookout tower. We were divided into the following crews: surveyors (five men), fallers (six men), buckers (six men), trimmers (ten men), a choker setter plus two others to help 'snake out' larger logs with a '60 Cat' (three men), a burning crew (ten men), a powder crew to blow out stumps and large rocks (two men), and the dozer crews with two '35 Cletracs,' one '50 Cat,' and, lastly, the '60 Cat' back pulling grader.

"On September 15, this work came to a sudden halt, when we, along with other camps in Washington, Oregon, and California, received a call for fire duty near Crescent City, California, and Bandon, Oregon.

"The town of Bandon already had burned to the ground when we arrived. For a month, we stayed on the fire line every day from 4:00 in the morning until around 7:00 in the evening. We finally finished our work on October 15. Then we were sent back to Fort Lewis for reassignment. Meanwhile, Company 4771 from Minnesota took over Camp Taneum.

Camp Quilcene, October 1936 to April 1937

"I next was assigned to the 'Fire Fightin' Fools' of Camp Quilcene, F-19, on Hood Canal, but my things had been sent to Camp Darrington in the north Cascades, so I was a little short of clothes for awhile. I was given a job 'falling snags' in a large burned over area. The trees on the Olympic Peninsula, of course, are very large; some stumps were ten feet across, and it took two of us to fall one of them.

"Typically, a truck took us to the foot of a mountain and dropped us off in three man crews. We hiked uphill about an hour, loaded down with a saw, two axes, a pair of wedges, two springboards, lunches, drinking water, and a gallon of mixed gas and oil to help loosen the saw if it became stuck in a stump.

"That November, some of us were sent to a side camp at Forks to construct roads. This was rough, thickly forested country. The only way we could hack out a road was by using a donkey engine, spar tree, and main line—with a 3/8 inch hand back line.

"I was a helper on a 'diesel Cat,' one of the first used in the CCC. It was started with a two horsepower gasoline engine mounted on the side. After the gas motor warmed the big engine, the diesel oil was turned on and the clutch was thrown in to turn the diesel motor over. If the machinery was warm enough, it started.

Camp Naches, October 1938 to May 1939

"Captain Osborne and Ensign Leon were the reserve officers in charge of Camp Naches when I arrived there. Leon also managed the baseball team, which played other camps and town teams.

"At Naches, I worked in the camp's little sawmill. Here, logs brought in on our small truck were cut into lumber for park benches, which we constructed at the site. Some of these tables remain in use today in campgrounds and parks in the Naches River area. The six feet long tables, weighing 300 pounds, were built with three inch planks, tempered by a coating of oil burned on with a hot iron.

"My next assignment was at the Raven Roost side camp, where I served as a cook's helper. Here, we built a road to a lookout tower. I left this camp and the CCC in May 1939."

Victor Snyder; Joining in the Early Days, 1933

As recounted in chapter four, Victor Snyder served with Company 945, which established Camp Sunset in 1933. He now is retired, living in Walla Walla, Washington. Following is his exceptional account about how he enlisted in the CCC:

"I will give a little background information as to why I joined the CCC in 1933, during the worst days of the Great Depression. For about four years, I had been working as a 'boat puller' salmon fisherman on the Columbia River for a man from Kelso. I also worked for him during the smelt run.

"In 1933, when we went upriver to Vancouver to our usual fishing grounds, we found out that the canneries were offering only six cents a pound for spring Chinook salmon that year. At that rock-bottom price, it was not worth it to even bother 'to get the nets wet.' The normal operating costs for twine, rope, and other supplies would eat up what little money could be made selling the catch. The local fishermen went home.

"I went back to Kelso, where I lived with my mother and two younger brothers. My dad had died a year and a half earlier, so they were without a means of support, and it had been up to me to provide for the family.

"I knew a man named Wilson, who was the employment manager at a local sawmill, and I talked to him about going to work there. He said that there might be a job available on the following Monday. He then gave me a slip of paper to take to the hospital for a physical examination, telling me that if a job opened up I would have a chance to get it. I would work three six-hour days a week. I asked about the wages they were paying; it was twenty-five cents an hour, which would total only $4.50 a week.

"I had no means of transportation except walking, so I started strolling back towards Kelso, and stopped at the hospital to take the physical examination. On the way, I started thinking about this new organization called the CCC, which was just starting up. A welfare department had recently opened in Kelso, and I knew the lady who was in charge. So, I 'barged in' to see her, asked her about joining the CCC, and told her my circumstances.

"It was a Wednesday, and she said that there would be a quota of twenty men from Cowlitz County going into the CCC next Saturday morning, but she thought all the openings already were filled. But, 'lo and behold,' that Friday I received a letter ordering me to report Saturday morning, June 3, 1933, to enroll in the CCC.

"Luckily, I was one of the twenty men from Cowlitz County sent to Vancouver Barracks for 'indoctrination' before assignment to Camp Sunset."

Joseph F. Schaffhauser, Sr.; From New York

From 1939 to 1941, Joseph F. Schaffhauser was an enlistee in the CCC. He was with Company 1297, from New York, while serving a year in the state of Washington. The company was assigned to summer camps in the central Cascades at Kachess Lake, Keechelus Lake, and Bumping Lake. Their winter camp was at Zillah.

Joseph now is retired, and lives in Mantour Falls, New York. In 1979, he traveled out West to visit his old CCC haunts. According to Joseph, the boys from New York learned a lot while in the forests of the Pacific Northwest:

"In April 1941, nine of us were sent ahead to Bumping Lake to set things up for when the rest of the company would arrive.

On Memorial Day, with nothing else to do, five of us set out on a hike. It was a beautiful day.

"After a couple of hours, two of the boys said that they were going to turn around and go back to camp. I told them to head for Copper Creek and follow it down; they would not have any problems finding the camp since it was located downstream. The three of us then went on, climbing one peak after another.

"As it started getting late, we noticed a building over on the next mountain, so we headed for it. When we finally got there, we discovered that it was a boarded up ranger station. We crawled through a window, finding inside only an old oil stove and a bed with no mattress. We got the stove going, and, being tired and wet from a full day out in the snow, we decided to spend the night there.

"We did not think that anyone at camp would worry about us, because the two boys that had gone back would let them know where we were going. After spending the night in the cabin, we started back to camp early the next morning in high spirits.

"Taking a different route down out of the mountains proved less tiresome. While on the trail, closer to camp, we happened to meet one of the guys who had stayed at Bumping Lake while we were on our outing. He was nearly in tears because we had not returned to camp the night before, nor, surprisingly, had our two companions who turned around the day before. The boys remaining in camp were so worried that they had called the supervisors, and a search party had been organized that morning to begin looking for all five of us.

"After my two companions and I had been back at camp for a couple of hours, the other two boys were finally found. They were in practically the same spot where we had left them. They had seen a bear, and were afraid to go on. After this incident, we had orders not to leave camp.

"Early in June 1941, I was sent down to the main camp, and, later the same month, I was on my way to Fort Dix, New Jersey, and home. These were two wonderful years for me. Soon after returning to the East, I landed a job with the federal government. I retired in March 1980.

"In recent years, it was a real high point in my life when I was able to return to the Pacific Northwest with my son and his wife, and visit the lakes of the central Cascades and the site of my old company's winter camp near Zillah."

Myer Schaffner; From Illinois to Northeast Washington, 1938

From his hometown of Waukegan, Illinois, near Chicago, Myer Schaffner signed up for a six month enlistment (July 1938 to January 1939), and was sent to the Colville National Forest in northeast Washington. Today he makes his home in Denver, Colorado:

"The nearest town to our camp was Kettle Falls, located twenty-five to thirty miles away. We were completely isolated, and the occasional trips into Colville or Marcus for a Saturday night dance (in the back of a canvas covered Army truck) were long and cold.

"Our job was to cut out dead tree snags and build new roads. The area had been devastated by forest fires ten years earlier, and the Forest Service was trying to open it up for sheep grazing.

"Most of the boys in our camp came from large cities in the East: New York, Philadelphia, etc. I believe we were the first company to occupy this camp, which we called 'Little America.' Imagine, if you can, young men who had never been out of the city working in an unbelievable forest of twisted dead trees.

"The tools we worked with were double-bitted axes, two-man saws, steel wedges, and sledges, and we wore spiked logger boots. At 'a dollar a day,' we earned our pay.

"I was a fat kid when I arrived, but it took just six weeks to lose twenty pounds. As a whole, the city boys were a rough lot. Somehow, each one found his 'niche,' and, in a short while, we were a hard working, responsible, and cohesive outfit. Our leaders were an Army captain and a lieutenant, who ran the camp. Two Forest Service men ran the jobs, and we had a camp doctor.

"It was dangerous work, and we learned about 'widow-makers' and splintering trees. There were some injuries, but no one was killed.

"After several months, I was 'promoted' to the dynamite crew. We blew the rocks and big stumps out of the right of way for new roads. Certainly, this was not kid's stuff!

"Orson Welles' broadcast of *War of the Worlds* on Sunday evening, October 30, 1938, created panic at our snowed in, isolated camp. The boys from New York and New Jersey were crying and screaming. [Welles' fictionalized, but believable, newscasts of a Martian invasion, of course, supposedly were originating from the northeast United States.] It was an unforgettable scene!

"In the winter of 1938-1939, there was too much snow and it was too cold to cut timber and build roads. Duties were shifted, and I spent my last two months in the CCC's as an 'Assistant Educational Advisor.' I guess I learned more than anyone else."

J. D. McReynolds; After Leaving the CCC

McReynolds' story about the CCC camps at Goldendale and Naches was related in chapter seven. As with many enrollees, he later served in the armed forces during World War II. Former CCC men, accustomed to barracks life and toughened by outdoor work, made a substantial contribution to America's ultimate victory over the Axis:

"After I got out of the 3C's, I worked at Yakima's Condon Orchards until 'Uncle Sam' wanted me. I was sent to Fort Douglas, Utah, just outside of Salt Lake City, and boarded a troop train to Camp McCain, Mississippi. There, I was part of a new military police outfit being formed, called the 408 M. P. E. G. C., and we took our basic training.

"We were first assigned to Camp Weingarten, Missouri, a prisoner of war camp. Then we were sent to Camp Perry, Ohio, located on the banks of Lake Erie, where the FBI conducts its target practice. There the company broke up, and I received orders to report to Camp Butner, North Carolina, then to Fort Belvoir, Virginia, just outside of Washington, D. C., followed by Newport News, Virginia, and finally I was sent overseas as a replacement.

"At Naples, Italy, I joined the 19th Combat Engineers, supporting the 34th Infantry Division, which was on the front line fighting the Germans. The unit I was with often worked under smoke screens and in the dark to keep supplies flowing to the infantry.

"During the campaign, two of us—a soldier from A Company, and myself, from C Company—served as bulldozer operators. We built the approach to the first American floating pontoon bridge across the Po River in northern Italy. My outfit moved up into Austria at the time of the German capitulation.

"With the German surrender, we were ordered back to Leghorn, Italy, and five thousand of us loaded a boat to be shipped to the Pacific. We went through the Panama Canal and landed at Luzon in the Philippines. At the war's end, I came home on 'points.'

"Back in the Yakima area, I drove logging trucks, tankers, and lumber trucks for the next twelve years. I met my wife Alma at a soda fountain in 1958, and we were married later that year. Actually, it was the second time we had gotten to know each other; we first met in 1946.

"After driving a truck and trailer for several more years, hauling lumber to Seattle, I thought I wanted to go into business for myself. We bought a used car lot, operating it for several years before a service station located next door became available, which we leased.

"Automobile sales were not that good, so we built a car wash on the property. In 1970, we bought an oil company and quit the service station business altogether. In 1975, we purchased another oil company, and I continued to be involved in these businesses until I retired in 1985."

William D. Cameron; Bataan Veteran

William D. Cameron was born September 19, 1921, at Middleport, Ohio. On joining the CCC, he was sent, along with ten other boys, to the Pacific Northwest. After his initial CCC training, he served as a radio operator at camps in Oregon, as well as at the Vancouver Control Station at Vancouver Barracks. He also received other "on the job training" and attended surveying classes.

Bill lives in Yakima with his wife (she is the former Leona Ramsdell from Tacoma). They were married in 1956, and have six daughters and six grandchildren. Bill is president of the Disabled American Veterans, Chapter #8, Yakima, and a past president of Yakima Valley Chapter #39, of the NACCCA. In his spare time, he lectures on history at Yakima Valley College. Here are his reminiscences:

"In 1939, I joined the CCC in Columbus, Ohio, and was sent to Company 3503, Camp Arboretum, S-220, near Corvallis, Oregon. At the camp, I worked as a radio operator and a relief ambulance driver on night calls.

"In June 1940, I was transferred to Camp Redmond, Oregon, where I again served as a radio operator. Most of that summer was spent at Camp Wickiup, a side camp, where nearly everyone in the company worked on a dam building project.

"I was discharged from the CCC in December 1940, and, going directly into the Army, I was stationed at Fort Monmouth, New Jersey. At this post, recruits received training in military communications.

"Because of my previous experience in the CCC as a radio operator, I was assigned as an instructor for a time. Eventually, I was transferred to a new Aircraft Warning Company, which operated a recently adopted aircraft detection system.

"My company was sent to the Philippines in April 1941. There, the unit was split up into individual detachments of approximately forty men, and assigned to the various U. S. Army Air Corps landing fields. I was ordered to the Iba Zambes airstrip, located on the west coast of Luzon on the South China Sea, where I remained until the outbreak of war, on December 7, 1941.

"After the complete destruction of the Iba Zambes airfield by Japanese planes in the first hours of the assault on the Philippines, I was sent to Fort McKinley, in Manila, to take charge of the net control station at military headquarters.

"Then, on December 25, 1941, I was transferred to General Parker's 31st Infantry Division headquarters, stationed on Bataan. Due to my knowledge of the west coast of Luzon and the South China Sea, however, I was sent back into western Luzon to establish an observation and communication post behind enemy lines. From here, we reported on Japanese land and sea movements.

"In the latter part of February 1942, I was ordered to abandon the position and report back to headquarters. I was accompanied by what was left of a squad of Filipino infantrymen, who had manned the machine guns protecting our outpost. It took us about two weeks to penetrate through enemy lines back to Bataan—a trek of about 100 miles, mostly through jungle to avoid detection by Japanese troops.

"That spring, just before the surrender of Bataan, I was transferred over to Corregidor Island in Manila Bay and assigned to the communications center. There, I remained on duty through twenty-seven days of continuous Japanese bombardment, until the island fortress finally fell in May 1942.

"After the surrender, the Japanese transferred a lot of captured military personnel, myself included, back to the Bataan Peninsula. It was here that the enemy perpetrated the infamous 'Bataan death march,' resulting in the cruel and unnecessary deaths of hundreds of prisoners of war. Five days later, after about 100 miles of forced marching under appalling conditions, what was left of our column reached prison quarters at Camp O'Donnell.

"Shortly, in June 1942, I was transferred along with a group of prisoners to Camp Cabanatuan, which was another 'hell hole.' I escaped, however, spending about six months in the mountains with Filipino guerillas, until I was turned in by pro-Japanese Filipinos.

"I was taken to Bilibid Prison in Manila, and court-martialed by the Japanese for not surrendering. I, along with two other Americans, was sentenced to what the Japanese called 'solitary confinement' for three years, and put in the old dungeon of a Spanish fort, which made up part of the historic old walled city in Manila. I remained in captivity there until a month prior to the invasion of Luzon by U. S. forces, which was in about April 1945. At that time, I was transferred back to Bilibid Prison.

"Upon my liberation by American soldiers, I weighed about 85 pounds, which was a little bit shy of my normal 150 pounds. I was placed on a hospital ship at Leyte, and transported back to Letterman General Hospital in San Francisco. After about a week there, I was transferred to a military hospital at Camp Attibury, Indiana.

"After about two weeks of examinations and treatment, I went home on a ninety day medical leave. After that period of time, I reported back to an Army Air Corps convalescent hospital at Fort George Wright in Spokane, Washington, until discharged from the armed forces."

Howard Clayton Hill; D-Day, June 6, 1944

My brother, "Clayton," seven years older than I, paid the full price for devotion to his country during World War II. Clayton, of course, had enrolled in the CCC in Georgia in the early 1930s, while I was still a youngster. His reports about life in the Civilian Conservation Corps were a major factor in my decision to join up in 1936, when I reached enlistment age.

During World War II, Clayton was a paratrooper in the Army's 82nd Airborne Division. Upon arriving in the British Isles, the 82nd prepared to play its part in the forthcoming Allied invasion of the continent.

Before D-Day, June 6, 1944, my brother and two buddies concluded a "pact" among themselves to watch out for each other. If one of them did not "make it," the survivors (or survivor) vowed to tell the story of how it happened to friends and relatives. As it turned out, just one of the three made it through the war.

In the darkness of night, prior to the massive seaborne landing by Canadian, British, and American troops that would come after daybreak, airborne divisions parachuted into the

Normandy countryside. As bad luck would have it, instead of infiltrating behind enemy lines as expected, the 82nd jumped right into the midst of German units. Enemy soldiers took up positions in the dark countryside, firing up at the descending paratroopers and inflicting many casualties.

As the one surviving member of the "pact" later related to my family, Clayton received a fatal wound while still in his harness, soaring down to the ground. Despite serious losses and the "bungled" nature of the parachute drop, the airborne divisions greatly disrupted German rear echelon areas, thus contributing significantly to the Allies' successful gain of a beach-head in France.

A. G. StJohn; From Florida

A. G. StJohn, a Floridian, received his CCC "indoctrination" in his home state before coming to the Pacific Northwest:

"I first became interested in the CCC when a camp was established at Ocean Pond, Florida (a freshwater lake about one mile wide), in the Osceola National Forest, some three miles from where I lived. As I was still in high school at the time, my interest in the CCC was only casual, although I did meet many of the enrollees from time to time, mostly in the local church. Many local girls, including one of my sisters, married boys from this camp.

"Finishing high school in 1936, I had hopes of receiving an appointment to the U. S. Naval Academy. Such was not to be the case, and, after working at many temporary jobs and being unable to accumulate enough money to enroll at the University of Florida, I decided in early 1937 that the CCC would be my best (and only) opportunity to make some small contribution to the welfare of my large family of brothers and sisters. We had been raised on my grandfather's farm, along with numerous cousins, aunts, and uncles, amid the usual hardships of the depression years.

"On January 15, 1937, a dozen or so local boys, myself included—all about seventeen or eighteen years of age—were loaded onto an Army truck and driven south to Green Cove Springs, Florida. There we boarded a train, and were told it would take us to Ohiopyle, Pennsylvania. From that point, we would be assigned to Company 5462, Camp Fort Necessity, SP-12, near Farmington, Pennsylvania.

"We were briefed about how cold we could expect it to be up North, and were issued the first of our CCC clothing—a short 'olive drab' Army overcoat. After an overnight ride, we arrived in Washington, D. C., where we had a half-day layover. We made good use of this time, jumping into a sight-seeing taxi (for a fare of about fifteen cents apiece), which took us on a grand tour of the White House, the Capitol building, the Washington Monument, and other sites.

"We ended up at a place called 'The States Restaurant' for lunch. Our driver informed us, probably 'tongue in cheek,' that it was a favorite dining place with the politicians.

"We boarded the train and continued our journey. Sometime in the early hours of the morning, we arrived at our destination, and were met by a truck from Fort Necessity. The truck took us out to the camp, where we were fed a hot meal and assigned to the barracks, while being offered much 'sympathy' for being in such a cold, desolate place.

"I had started a diary about the time I finished high school, and I noted in it on January 19, 1937: 'Having a job getting onto CCC routine and getting adjusted to Pennsylvania climate.' Also that winter, I was to make the frequent notation: 'No work today due to unsettled weather.'

"After being outfitted with clothing of World War I Army vintage, I was assigned to a crew doing road construction and maintenance work in Fort Necessity State Park. Our immediate supervisor at the time was 'Leader' Archie Odom, while the 'Foreman' was Paul McGill, who had been an Army captain in World War I.

"After I worked on this crew for a few days, it became known that I was a reasonably good typist, so I was assigned, along with another man named William C. West, to the 'guide service' at Fort Necessity. Our duties entailed maintaining the fort, escorting visitors, keeping a visitors' log, and doing routine office work for the park ranger, who was a lovely woman named Ruth H. Martin.

"Camp life at this time was also beginning to be more interesting, and we had opportunities for educational, social, recreational, and artistic development. There were instructional movies, health lectures, religious programs and services, camp dances, and trips to Uniontown. For the first time in my life, I attended a concert by a string quartet, which performed in the camp.

"While stationed at Fort Necessity, a highlight of our off duty hours was visiting an 'NYA' [National Youth Administration] girls' camp at Jumonville, Tennessee. I met many girls, some of whom I have continued to correspond with now for many years. Along with the work, there was time to relax and have fun.

"After being at Fort Necessity for half a year, we learned in July 1937 that Company 5462 would be disbanded. I was to be transferred to Company 5481, Camp Kooser, S-99, Somerset, Pennsylvania. This, to me, was traumatic, as I had just begun to settle into a nice routine. On July 25, however, I and some others arrived at Camp Kooser.

"I was assigned to work in the supply room, but, after a couple of days, the project superintendent offered a friend, Pat H. Lander, and I a chance to work in his office. This I enjoyed, and I began a crash program to learn how to fill out the various reports and do other routine office duties. Just as I was becoming effective, we were informed that the entire company would be moved to Camp Sunset, F-39, Yacolt, Washington.

"Our transcontinental trip by train went without incident, and we arrived at our destination, Camp Sunset. Little did I know at the time that our company was destined to be assigned to Washington's south Cascades for nearly three years." [StJohn's experiences at Camp Sunset and Camp Skamania already have been presented in chapter four.]

"After our long-term duty in the area, Company 5481 was disbanded at Camp Skamania on August 17, 1940, and I was transferred to Camp Summit, F-138, Government Camp, Oregon, in the shadow of Mt. Hood. About this time, not having been home or having seen any of my family since January 1937, I decided it was time to do something else. I applied for a discharge, and arrived home in Olustee, Florida, on September 28, 1940.

"In October 1940, however, being twenty-one years of age, I was one of the first in my town to register with the Selective Service. Being in fine physical shape due to my three years of CCC treatment, I naturally was put in class 1-A.

"At this time, I worked awhile as a civilian helping to build Camp Blanding, Florida. With the world situation being what it was in the early 1940s, and having had a life at sea in the back of my mind since high school days, I enlisted for a six year hitch in the U. S. Navy on May 20, 1941.

"After recruit training, I was assigned to hospital corps school, and eventually wound up in New Zealand in 1942, where I met and later married a lovely girl. After the war, having acquired a wife and advancing to 'Chief Petty Officer,' I decided to stay in the Navy.

"I was promoted to 'Master Chief Petty Officer' in 1960, was commissioned as a line officer in 1963, and retired with the rank of Lieutenant in 1971, after thirty years of service.

"When I reflect back upon my days in the CCC, I am struck by how young and impressionable all of us lads were at that time. Most of the CCC officers and others in supervisory positions were looked upon by me, and I am sure by others, as father figures.

"All my life, I have been eternally grateful that during my early years I knew such men—Captain J. Z. Amacker, Lieutenant Everett F. Ziegler, Major C. T. Waring, 'Foreman' Alex McKay, K. P. Cecil and Ryle Teed of the Forest Service, Ranger K. C. Langfield, and a host of others in CCC camps in Pennsylvania and Washington, who were my heroes, role models, teachers, and, most of all, my friends.

"They helped set me on what I think was the right path."

Appendix One

Camp Soda Springs Behavior Book

With the message on its cover— "Don't worry about what to do—READ this book and KNOW"— the Behavior Book reproduced here was given to new enlistees at Camp Soda Springs, located about thirty-five miles west of Yakima on the North Fork of Ahtanum Creek. This facility was occupied by Company 2942 from 1935 to 1939 (see chapter seven for the story of Camp Soda Springs).

Similar guide booklets and instructional pamphlets were distributed at other camps across the United States and the territories. The advice and regulations contained in the Camp Soda Springs Behavior Book *are typical, and excerpts taken from it give a good gleaning of what life was like for enrollees in the CCC:*

Camp Regulations

If everyone did just what he should do, there would be no need for regulations—but with human nature what it is today, the following regulations are given for all concerned with life in this camp, and that includes all members of this Co. 2942. They are for the good and benefit of all.

1. Drinking or possession of liquor within the area of this camp or in any Government vehicle is strictly forbidden.
2. All existing regulations are posted on the camp bulletin board, by the Company Office and in each barracks and ignorance of them is no excuse for breaking any of them . . .

Army Office Rules . . .

1. All enrollees will knock before entering the office.
2. Enrollees will come to the office on official business only and will depart as soon as completed . . .
4. The equipment in the Army office is for official use and no one will be permitted to use the typewriters, etc without permission of the Senior Leader.

Leave

Re-enrollment Leave.

1. Six day re-enrollment leave is granted each enrollee having completed a six months enrollment period, and must be taken within the following six months period, as it does not accumulate.

Emergency Leave.

2. Each enrollee accumulates 1 1/4 days of emergency leave each month and it may accumulate. This leave is only granted in cases of serious illness and death.
3. When an enrollee is granted either Re-enrollment or Emergency leave, he must first report to the office and sign the forms granting such leave. Upon signing these forms he reports to the Camp Doctor for a physical examination, and if he is in good health is permitted to leave camp with the first available transportation.

Week End Pass.

4. An enrollee is entitled to leave during the week end, providing he is not on the week-end roster, has all educational work completed and is granted permission to leave. Sufficient transportation is furnished to take all enrollees wishing to go to town each Saturday.
5. All enrollees leaving camp will be dressed in full O.D. uniform or in civilian clothes. Mixing of O.D. and civilian clothes will not be permitted . . .

Should an enrollee be absent on authorized leave, it will be the responsibility of those men sleeping next to the absent member to take care of his bed and personal belongings.

General

Barracks bags are to be used for the sole purpose of keeping dirty laundry. No other articles will be permitted in them.

The schedule for lights during the week is as follows:

Sunday to Thursday inclusive—
Tattoo at—9:15 P.M.
Taps and lights out—9:30 P.M.

Friday and Saturday—
Tattoo at—9:45 P.M.
Taps and lights out—10:00 P.M.

Retreat

At approximately 4:55 P.M. assembly will be sounded on the public address system and all enrollees will assemble in their assigned places on the road, facing the flag.

Uniform will consist of O.D. shirt, O.D. trousers, black tie and garrison shoes, well polished. Uniforms will be clean and neat at all times and enrollees will be clean shaven.

Retreat will be held on week days only.

General Formation for Mess

Enrollees will form in a line . . . and will not march to the Mess Hall until the bugle call of Mess is blown on the P.A. system.

The schedule for meals is as follows:

Monday to Friday—inclusive
Breakfast—6:30 A.M.
Dinner—12:00 Noon
Supper—5:00 P.M.

Saturday—
Breakfast—7:30 A.M.
Dinner—12:30 P.M.
Supper—5:00 P.M.

Sunday—
Breakfast—8:00 A.M.
Dinner—1:00 P.M.
Supper—5:00 P.M.

Regulations Governing Conduct at Mess

1. Observe quiet at all times.
2. No profane language will be tolerated.
3. Ask for the food—don't reach or grab.
4. Don't slop on tables or floor, but if an accident happens, wipe up all spilled liquids.
5. Only one man per table will be allowed at the serving counter at one time.
6. Think of the other fellows—Don't hog the food.
7. Carry your dishes, silverware, peelings, wrappers etc to the counter when through eating. Leave a clean table.
8. Handle dishes and silverware with care. Failure to do so will result in you paying for damage or breakage.
9. Eat slowly and chew your food thoroughly. Conduct yourself as a gentleman at all times.

Pay Rolls

Enrollees will be notified of the time and place of signing the payroll, which will be about the 19th of each month.

When appearing at the pay table, all men will dress in O.D. shirts, trousers, black ties and garrison shoes. Enrollees will be paid as their names are called—leaders and assistant leaders first and the other enrollees in alphabetical order . . .

Educational Requirements

Each enrollee is required to attend at least one hour of class work weekly, or carry at least one correspondence course, turning in one completed lesson weekly. This regulation will be complied with within one week of enrollment and maintained by each man until his discharge and includes all rated men of Junior classification . . .

Barracks Regulations

1. All beds will be placed alternately and against the wall . . .
5. Barracks bag will be tied to the end of the bed toward the aisle . . .
6. Barracks will be scrubbed out each week, fires will be built in barracks stoves when crews come in and will be kept going until just before "Lights Out" at which time the men in the barracks will fill the stoves and close the drafts. Night men will keep fires in barracks the remainder of the night until Reveille sounds the following morning . . .
8. Barracks leaders and assistants are responsible for the police and the interior and exterior of their respective barracks. They also are responsible for the actions and behavior of the men in their barracks.
9. All windows . . . will be left open during the day, on days when it is not actually snowing or raining.
10. Calked boots will never be worn in the barracks at any time . . .
11. No men will be permitted in the barracks while the crews are on the jobs . . .

Camp Dispensary

Emergencies will be taken care of at any time of the day or night. Sick call will be held as follows:

7:00 to 7:30 A.M.
5:30 to 6:00 P.M.

The Camp Surgeon, when in camp, will be present at sick call and may be called for other attention as needed. . .
First aid cards will be held by all First Aid attendants, Leaders, Assistant Leaders, Project Assistants, and Truck Drivers. Instruction will be available to all enrollees desiring and willing to attend the full number of classes . . .

Project Work

The Camp Superintendent is directly responsible for all work done on the project and for all enrollees turned over to him by the Army, for work on the project. At all other times the enrollee is under the direct supervision of the Company Commander.
The Technical Service has an overhead similar to that of the Army. It consists of a Camp Clerk, Tool Clerk, Assistant Mechanic, Blacksmith and others.

The majority of the enrollees are turned over to the Technical Service for work in the field. They are divided into crews under the supervision of a foreman, who again divides his crew into groups under Leaders and Assistant Leaders, and assigns them to various jobs under his supervision . . .

Physical Training

Physical training exercises will be conducted every morning except Saturday and Sunday.

Formation will be in the retreat area at 6:15 A.M.

This formation is mandatory.

No enrollee will be absent without the permission of the Commanding Officer or the Senior Leader . . .

Fire Drill

A fire drill will be held at least once a week, and will be of a surprise nature.

Enrollees will learn their positions and the equipment that they are to take to the fire, and will assume those positions upon first hearing the siren.

Conduct of All Enrollees . . .

1. The word "Sir" will be used in addressing an officer or member of the technical service.
2. When an officer enters a building where the enrollees are present, they will immediately arise and come to attention, and will remain at attention until further directed by the officer.
3. In the case of camp inspections by any visiting officers or the Area Inspector, the members of the company overhead on duty, will immediately come to attention and will then introduce themselves by name and station, as follows: "Enrollee Eaton, Assistant Educational Advisor, Sir" . . .

"If you are wrong, you can't afford to argue; if you are right, you don't need to!"

Appendix Two

Barracks Writers

WHAT MIGHT HAVE BEEN
(To Mr. Roosevelt)
By Raymond Kraus
Co. 1232, Olympia, Wash.

A pauper's life we might have led,
And died revolting for our bread;
We might have shed each other's blood,
And died face down within the mud.

But all because we have this man,
Whose only words are there: "I can!"
Our nation shall evolve on high,
And we shall see a brighter sky.

He gave to us the chance to say,
I've earned my bread and keep today,
The chance to smile, to toil, to sweat,
This damn depression thus forget.

Happy Days, November 3, 1934 (national
newspaper of the CCC, Washington, D. C.)

THE WAIL OF A SPIKE CAMPER
By R. F. McMahon, Co. 1744
Avery, Idaho

I joined a brand new outfit
They called it the CCC
They issued me my clothing
And put three shots in me.
They sent me out to a spike camp
Put a cot beneath my frame
They gave me a thousand-pound hammer
And a pick to go with same.
They fed me mush and eggs and bacon
I never got to town
It looks to me like I'm a sucker
Until my time runs down.

Happy Days, May 25, 1935

MY PACKSACK
By Joe Werner, Co. 932
Naches, Wash.

What does my packsack hold, you ask?
Well, of what does the sky consist?
What is the length of a week-end hike[?]
And why does the morning mist?

Why is a glacier green and cold?
What do you think of the moon?
When is a bear too close and too bold?
And what is the cry of a loon?

How many years is a mountain goat[']s life?
Are there insects that live in the snow?
Does an eagle spin in his flight?
And where does the Juniper grow?

Take a look inside my packsack friend,
For in it I can carry the earth.
There's room for the wind and
  one sun and the sky,
And a little pocket for mirth.

Happy Days, July 29, 1933

ODE TO AN A.W.O.L.
By Herron Dawson
Co. 1974, Centerville, Idaho

Over the hill to the sunny side;
Back where the clover grows,
Up the gulch and across the creek;
That's where the welcher goes.

The hours speed past and the sun goes down;
And the chill of the night so black;
Is worse than the chill in a CC bunk;
So the welcher ambles back.

No more he'll stray from the better way;
No more shall he try to roam,
He'll work, no doubt, 'till his hitch is out,
And ride the cushions home.

Happy Days, July 20, 1935

THE CCC PRISONER'S SONG
A parody on "The Prisoner's Song"
By C. S. Woods, Co. 1922, [WWI veterans]
S-220, Corvallis, Ore.

We are going to a new fire tomorrow,
To make trails o'er the mountains and humps[;]
There'll be tall burning snags all 'round us
And at night we'll be guarding the stumps.

We are prisoners, because of these fires;
Can't leave camp, cannot go anywhere . . .

Every year there's a new conflagration,
There's a new one to threaten some town;
Every year there are thousands of acres
Left smoldering, just dead on the ground . . .

We'll be going to a new fire tomorrow . . .

Happy Days, October 16, 1937

WORTH IT
By Doc Towne
Co. 615, Estacada, Ore.

My hands are sore an' blistered, boys,
My bones are full of aches;
My elbow joints, they make a noise
Like an ungreased windmill makes.

How come? I been a choppin' trees,
A-hewin' logs and such;
The kind of work that pleases
A C.C.C. very much.

I've got a bunk and windows, too,
With one that's set just right;
For us to watch the moon rise
When work is through at night.

That ax has sure wore out my hand,
But, boys, my heart ain't sore;
I'll stand her there to meet me
Just out the bunkhouse door.

But I've been at it jest the same,
An' up Clackamas Valley Draw;
Now stands Company 615
Best of them all.

Happy Days, September 22, 1934

Appendix Three

History of Fort Lewis CCC District

The following excellent account is excerpted from the Official Annual—Fort Lewis District Civilian Conservation Corps Ninth Corps Area, 1937, *pp. 22-27. It reveals the rapidity with which the mobilization of enrollees and supervisory personnel occurred when the CCC was established in the spring of 1933. The departments of Labor, Agriculture, and Interior, and the Army proved flexible and adaptable as circumstances demanded when setting up the CCC organization.*

Scores of CCC "districts" were formed across the nation within each of the Army's nine military "Corps Areas." The Fort Lewis District, as well as the Vancouver Barracks District, the Fort George Wright District (headquarters, Spokane), and the Lewiston District (headquarters, Lewiston Normal School, now LCSC, Lewiston, Idaho), was administered by the Ninth Army Corps Area. Altogether, the Ninth Corps encompassed the states of Washington, Idaho, California, Oregon, Montana, Wyoming, and Utah—containing fifteen CCC districts in 1936.

The first enrollees in the Fort Lewis District were of high caliber; however, the clothing and equipment that were issued to them was inferior, as this excellent account reveals. Much of it was of World War I vintage, often worn out from overuse or age. The early enrollees had toes poking out of GI issue boots, while ancient Liberty trucks, having a top speed of 15 mph, often broke down or bogged down on trips to the new camps. Better quality clothes and newer equipment, of course, eventually were issued.

Here, then, are excerpts from the historical section of the Fort Lewis District Annual, *describing important events from the founding of the CCC in 1933 up to the year 1937:*

. . . The first letter to be received by Headquarters, Fort Lewis, Washington, pertaining to CCC activities was an immediate action letter from Ninth Corps Area, dated April 8, 1933, and designated as "CCC Letter No. 1." In this communication the general provisions. . .were set down including the information that:

a. Enrollees of the Civilian Conservation Corps were to be selected by the United States Department of Labor.

b. The War Department was charged with the responsibility of organization, control, transportation, maintenance—the housing, rationing, allotting, equipping, medical attention, and payment.

c. Three Regular Army Posts in Western Washington were detailed the job of organizing enrollees for this organization into companies.

Fort Lewis, responsible for enrolling 2,800 men,

Fort Worden, responsible for enrolling 800 men,

Fort Lawton, responsible for enrolling 200 men.

d. All existing facilities found at these three posts were definitely to be utilized in this organization work.

e. Members of the CCC, while under War Department control, were not subject to Articles of War.

About April 12, 1933, the decision was made to utilize Reserve Officers in this line of duty.

CCC Letter No. 21, dated May 3, 1933, was received . . . to organize specific companies as follows:

Fort Lewis [companies 930, 931, 932, 933, 934, 944, 945, 963, 964, 965, 966, 982, and 983] . . .

Fort Worden [near Port Townsend; companies 936, 937, 946, and 947] . . .

Fort Lawton [Seattle; companies 935 and 948] . . .

During this organization period Regular Army Officers were reconnoitering sites proposed by the Technical Services for occupation by these work companies. The locations finally decided upon for camps during the first period, 1933, and the companies designated for same were:

Company	Camp	Company	Camp
266.	Deception Pass	1232.	Narada
697.	Upper Cispus	1235.	Moran
930.	Longmire	1234.	Ahtanum
931.	Icicle	1622.	Pack Forest
932.	Currant Flat	1624.	Abernathy Mountain
933.	Lower Cispus	1626.	Matlock
934.	Darrington	1627.	Leland
935.	Boulder	1629.	Lester
936.	Elwha	1630.	Glacier
937.	Easton	1631.	Carbon White River
946.	Quilcene	1632.	Snider
947.	Lake Cushman	1633.	Carbon River
982.	Humptulips	1634.	Hamilton (Lyman)
983.	Mineral	1635.	Skykomish
1228.	Tieton	1636.	Skagit
1229.	White River	1638.	Beehive
1230.	Salmon La Sac	1639.	Randle
1231.	Upper West Side Highway	1640.	Naselle
		1923.	Sultan [Washington WWI veterans]

These companies included thirteen Ninth Corps Area Companies organized in this state as well as sixteen Sixth Corps Area Companies [Michigan, Wisconsin, and Illinois] and eight Second Corps Area Companies [New York, New Jersey, and Delaware] that came in to this District from the East. [The Corps

Area in which a company was first formed was indicated by the third digit from the right in a company's number.]

The first Reserve Officers to report for duty in connection with the CCC at Fort Lewis arrived the evening of May 2, 1933, and were assigned their duties May 3rd. At this same time officers were also reporting at Fort Worden and Fort Lawton. The original organization facilities for the CCC included a tent conditioning camp established near the present site of the football field on the Post at Fort Lewis and under command at this time, of the Regular Army.

By May 2, 1933, about 250 enrollees were on hand at this conditioning camp. Regulations and proper procedures were unknown. No supplies or equipment were available, and what things were used were borrowed from the Regular Army, who furnished what they had on hand. Reserve officers, supervising these activities, were for the first time on active duty and new to this type of work.

From the date May 2nd on, men arrived every hour or so in groups of from fifty to seventy-five. They arrived without any advance warning and were generally cold, unfed, and poorly clad. This influx of recruited enrollees continued until 2,500 men were in the tent conditioning camp, representing the peak of the organization activities.

Life in the conditioning camps was more or less one of orientation, light work, and the usual run of shots for typhoid and smallpox.

The tent floors of the Fort Lewis conditioning camp were made from lumber turned out on the post from timber once standing on the reservation. Every once in a while a bright, metal-looking spot would appear, and upon investigation a piece of a bullet or shell would be found. The CCC enrollees had to construct their own latrines, but later the conditioning camp was hooked on to the old war-time post sewer system. Clothing issued was stock stored on the Post since 1917. Old style, war-time made, and because of its long storage, it deteriorated rapidly, especially the shoes, which, at times would only last long enough for the enrollee to wear them from the issue room to his tent.

During the period of the tent conditioning camp at Fort Lewis bathing facilities were practically non-existent. Permission was secured to use the old swimming pool at Green Park and an odd sight it was to see 250 men with towels around their necks (mobbing) along the highway with a reserve officer to go bathing.

It was also the custom at this time to give the men two or three hours' walk to keep them occupied, and a company would string out at route march for quite a distance, spending a morning or afternoon covering a portion of the vast Fort Lewis reservation.

Shortly after May 2, 1933, at the conditioning camp, companies with a strength of 250 men were formed, with a Regular Army Officer in command, two Reserve Officers as Junior Officers, Army enlisted personnel for Mess Stewards, and sometimes cooks.

The departure for the woods of the first few companies . . . was noted with great interest. The first company to move out was the 930th CCC Company which went to Longmire [Mt. Rainier National Park] under the command of Lieut. Beadle, 6th Eng., on May 15, 1933. Perhaps we should say that the cadre moved out on the 15th and the company the next day. In some cases the company caught up with the cadre before reaching the camp site. Old Liberty trucks, governed at fifteen M. P. H., with hard rubber tires were the only transportation available, and these were frequently mired down on the mountain roads. Some trucks arrived in camp with two or three others in tow. Later a shipment of old abandoned postal trucks was received, but few, if any, of these lasted one round trip to the camp.

And so it was that, from such a conditioning camp and under these conditions the members of the first CCC Company, slowly made their way in convoy to the paradise of nature lovers, Longmire . . . Here the 250 embryo CCC members disembarked, and the establishment of their camp, with tents lining the company streets, was completed. Work crews soon were organized and details, under National Park Service supervision, carried on an efficient and outstanding work program.

On May 16, 1933, CCC Company 933, commanded by Capt. J. R. Williams, with First Lieut. Harold Liebe as Junior Officer, moved out to Camp Lower Cispus, the first camp started as a permanent camp. The construction of this camp was accomplished wholly by CCC labor. No civilian carpenters were used, and the camp was completed in July, 1933.

From time to time during this First Period, camps moved out to their locations—some of them to tent camps, others to permanent ones. Camps Darrington, Lake Cushman, and Lower Cispus were the only camps built permanently during the First Period . . .

From the First Period (April, 1933) to the present time [1937], the numbers of companies in this District fluctuated in keeping with the need for employment, reaching a "high" of fifty-four camps during the Fifth Period (1935), and now including during the Tenth Period (1937) a total of twenty-nine camps . . .

During the first few weeks of January, 1935, Western Washington received a heavy blanket of snow. One of the warm winds peculiar to this country, called "Chinook," sprang up, the blanket of snow quickly turned to water, streams became swollen and raging torrents, in many cases leaving their banks and sweeping everything before them. Several camps on the Olympic Peninsula were soon isolated and in some cases even flooded. Fort Lewis District Headquarters learned of the plights of these camps by amateur radios getting messages through as all other means of communication were cut off; getting food supplies, etc., to camps became a problem.

Convoys were started out with supplies, one even became marooned when near its destination—supplies to Clearwater were taken in by Indians using canoes. Fortunately no lives were lost, camps not seriously damaged, and time and work soon erased traces.

In October, 1936, when smoke of a big forest fire in southwestern Oregon was visible in neighboring states hundreds of miles from the conflagration which was covering thousands of blackened acres, the Fort Lewis District was called on to reinforce the large army of fighters already battling the stubborn and terrible blaze [i. e., the Bandon fire].

Five hundred and fifty Ninth Corps Area men in this District were mustered from eight camps . . . Icicle, Naches, Darrington, Taneum, Quilcene, North Bend, Snider, and Lake . . . Cushman . . . and sent by truck to Fort Lewis to entrain for Oregon . . .

Several motor pool convoys were rushed to the district warehouse at Fort Lewis for fire-fighting equipment. Headquarters clerks were called on for over-time duty to outfit this fire army.

. . . [The] Washington State Patrol, assisted the CCC motor convoys during their long drive to the fire site . . . and greatly aided the trucks to reach their destination without loss of time or danger of mishap.

A special fast train from Fort Lewis hurried the several officers and necessary supervisory overhead, together with the men, south to the fire front.

Towns were consumed, lives lost and danger lay in all directions; the roaring tongues of flame at first could not be checked, stopping the fire seemed out of the question. The work of hundreds of weary fighters from the three states of Oregon, California and Washington seemed to avail little until a heavy 1,500-foot fog blanket came to help.

Word was received at District Headquarters at Fort Lewis that the fires in Oregon were all under control on December 7th, and that rain in the past week had relieved that danger that threatened the forests . . .

The work accomplished by the CCC enrollees . . . under the supervision of the Technical Agencies, has been outstanding . . . agencies . . . represented in camps in this District . . . are classified as follows:

National Forestry Camps [e. g., Camp Naches, F-70]

State Forestry and Private Camps [e. g., Camp Sultan, S-236, and Camp Electron, P-201]

State Parks Camps [e. g., Camp Lewis and Clark, SP-2]

National Parks Camps [e.g., Camp Ohanapecosh, NP-6]

Soil Conservation Camps [e. g., Camp Soda Springs, SCS-6]

Bureau of Reclamation Camps [e.g., Camp Zillah, BR-58]

[Department of War Camps; e. g., Camp Lewis, A-1]

[In] Announcing that the last three years [1934-1937] have shown the lowest forest-fire losses ever recorded in such a period in the Pacific Northwest, the United States Forestry Service gives deserved credit to the CCC . . .

"Fire hazard has been reduced on thousands of acres and hundreds of miles of fire-break have made the danger of uncontrolled blazes less imminent," the Forestry Service reports.

The figures speak even more forcefully. The fire loss inside of national forest boundaries in Oregon and Washington during the past three years was 20,802 acres. Prior to 1933, when the CCC was established, the lowest three-year loss was 84,000 acres.

Beyond this material accomplishment which the foresters praise, the building of trails and the saving of trees, is the service of the Civilian Conservation Corps in building morale and saving manhood . . .

Selected References

Carroll, Robert Wesley. "The Civilian Conservation Corps in Washington State 1933-1942." M. A. thesis, Washington State University, Pullman, 1973.

The Fort George Wright District Civilian Conservation Corps Annual, 1937, and *1938-39* [Spokane]; and *Pictorial Review, Civilian Conservation Corps, Fort George Wright District* [1940?]. [see Jay Mark Gleason Papers, Manuscripts, Archives, and Special Collections, Washington State University, Pullman; also for outstanding authentic color slides of CCC activities, circa late 1930s/early 1940s in Washington state, see Arthur Earl Victor collection]

Hansen, Mel. *Southwest Washington Cascades Indian Heaven Back Country: Trails, Lakes and Indian Lore.* Beaverton, Oregon: Touchstone, 1977.

Howell, Glenn. *C.C.C. Boys Remember: A Pictorial History of the Civilian Conservation Corps.* Medford, Oregon: Klocker, 1976.

Lacy, Leslie Alexander. *The Soil Soldiers: The Civilian Conservation Corps in the Great Depression.* Radnor, Pennsylvania: Chilton, 1976.

The Lewis-Clark Broad Axe, 1935-1936. Lewiston District, Civilian Conservation Corps, Lewiston, Idaho, 1936. [provided by courtesy of John Wies]

Official Annual—Fort Lewis District Civilian Conservation Corps Ninth Corps Area, 1937. Fort Lewis District, December 1937. [provided by courtesy of Edward Hayes]

Official Annual—Vancouver Barracks Civilian Conservation Corps Ninth Corps Area, 1937. Vancouver Barracks CCC District, January 1, 1938. [provided by courtesy of Sam Keikkala]

Perkins, Frances. *The Roosevelt I Knew.* New York: Viking, 1946.

Roosevelt, Eleanor. *This I Remember.* New York: Harper and Brothers, 1949.

Rosenman, Samuel I., Ed. *The Public Papers and Addresses of Franklin D. Roosevelt, Volume Two, The Year of Crisis 1933.* New York: Random House, 1938.

Salmond, John A. *The Civilian Conservation Corps, 1933-1942: A New Deal Case Study.* Durham, North Carolina: Duke University Press, 1967.

Throop, Elizabeth Gail. "Utterly Visionary and Chimerical: A Federal Response to the Depression—An Examination of Civilian Conservation Corps Construction on National Forest System Lands in the Pacific Northwest." M. A. thesis, Portland State University, Oregon, 1979.

Index

A

Abbott, Arthur "Powerhouse," 105
Amacker, Captain J. Z., 168
American Red Cross, 19
American River ski lodge, 103, *148*
Anderson, Celo, 47, 84
Anderson, L. H., 126
Arneson, Arnold, 127
Arnold, Fred, 36, 45, 76, 79

B

Baily, Captain William, 125, 127
Barger, Velma. *See* Hill, Velma Barger
Beacon Rock State Park, 106-107
Brown, Donald, *146*, 154-156
Bureau of Indian Affairs, 93, 129

C

Cameron, William D., 161-164
Carlan, Fred, 6
Cassidy, Thomas, 105
Cecil, K. P., 168
Cispus burn, 110
Cispus Environmental Learning Center, 111
Cispus River, 57, 109-111
Civilian Conservation Corps—CCC (Washington and U. S.)
  accomplishments, 71, 99, 100, 103, 104, 107, 108, 110-111, 124-126, 127-128, 132-133, 135-136, 138-141. *See Also* CCC camps
  barracks life, 27-28, 47, 118-119
CCC camps, 26, 70, 89-90, 117-118
Camp Beacon Rock, 106-107
Camp, Big Meadow (Virginia), *22*
Camp Columbia, *134*, 141
Camp Cherry Valley, 100
Camp Cougar, 12, 89-93
Camp Darrington, *147*, 155
Camp Deception Pass, 113-114, 115
Camp Electron, *152*

Camp Fort Necessity (Pennsylvania), *148*, 166, 167
Camp Ginkgo, 103-104, 105
Camp Goldendale, 44-45, 99, 120
Camp Hard Labor Creek (Georgia), 11, 23-26, 29, 32, 33, 38, 53
Camp Hemlock, 49, 81, 107-109, *146*
Camp Kooser (Pennsylvania), 167
Camp Lewis and Clark, 115
Camp Lookout Mountain, 109
Camp Lower Cispus, 74-75, 109-111
Camp Moran, 114, 123-127, *147*
Camp Naches, 99-101, 103, *148*, 155-156
Camp Nehalem (Oregon), 131
Camp Nile, 99
Camp North Bend, 121-123
Camp Ostrich Bay, 111-112, 113, 121
Camp Quilcene, 155
Camp Rehers (Oregon), 131
Camp Saltwater, 101, 103, 105
Camp Shafer Butte (Idaho), *144*, *145*
Camp Skamania, 11-12, 58, *63*, *66*, 69-72, 74, 79, 81, 86, 167
Camp Soda Springs, 117-121
Camp Summit (Oregon), 167
Camp Sunset, 11, 40, 42, 43-47, 49, 50-52, 54-56, 58, *60*, 85, *149*, 156-157, 167
Camp Taneum, *146*, 154-155
Camp Tieton, 127-128
Camp Trask (Oregon), 131
Camp Upper Cispus, 110
Camp Waterville, 120
Camp Winfield Scott (Virginia), 106
Camp Zig Zag (Oregon), 132-133
Camp Zillah, 98, 157, 159

CCC companies, 36, 98
Company 290 (Camp Shafer Butte, Idaho), *144*
Company 350 (Big Meadow Camp, Virginia), *22*
Company 603 (Tyee Springs vicinity), *150*
Company 697, 109
Company 928 (Camp Zig Zag, Oregon), 132-133
Company 932 (Camp Naches), 99-101, 103, *148.*
Company 933, 109
Company 935 (Camp Ginkgo), 103, 105
Company 944 (Camp Hemlock), 107-109, *146*
Company 945 (Camps Sunset and Goldendale), 43-45, 56, 57, 99
Company 1233 (Camp Moran), 123-125, *147*
Company 1297 (Camp Zillah), 98, 157
Company 1639, 109
Company 1650 (Camp Tieton), 127
Company 2911 (Camp North Bend), 121-123
Company 2919 (Camp Lower Cispus), 109-111
Company 2942 (Camp Soda Springs), 117-120
Company 3224 (Camp Ginkgo), 105
Company 3442 (Camp Hard Labor Creek, Georgia), 11
Company 4768 (Camp Moran), 125-127
Company 4769 (Camp Tieton), 127-128
Company 4771 (Camp Taneum), 155
Company 4786 (Camp Ostrich Bay, etc.), 111-114, 121
Company 5480 (Camp Beacon Rock), 106-107

Company 5481 (Camp Sunset), 11, 45-46, 71, *149*, 167
discharge, 33, 85
educational opportunities, 52-53, *66*, 101, 113, 127, 137
enlistment, 23-25, 33, 36
entertainment and recreation, 50-52, 58-59, 78-80, 85-86, *88*, 90-91, 100, 101, 105, 106, 109, 112, 117, 120, 124, 127, 157-159
fire fighting, 42-43, *68*, 70, 72, 74-75, 81-83, 121, 122, 128, 130-132
floods, 43, 57-58, 139
historical restoration, 140
Indian Division, 128-130
mascots, *66*, 91-92, 129-130
meals, 31-32, 51, 90, 119, 122-123
newspapers
  Happy Days, *22*, 101, 126, 153
  Landscaper, 120
  Missouri Wanderer, 113
  Petrified Paragraphs, 105
  Progress, 105
  Saltwater Seagull, 101, 105
  War Whoop, 101
rescues, 76, 111, 113, 122
soil conservation, 26, 31, 44, *96*, 99, 106, 119, 139, 141, *149, 151*
termination, 137-138
Cleaver, Lieutenant Louis, 118
Columbia National Forest, 42, 43, 58, 83, 89, 107, *150*
Colville Indian Reservation, 128
Colville National Forest, 159
Connor, Paul, *148*
Cowlitz River, 43, 57, 110

D

Davidson, Captain Arthur, *149*
Davis, Jessie, 53, *66*
Deception Pass State Park, 113-114
Dietz, Joe, *148*
Doyal, Gregory, *148*
Dozier, Rex, *148*
Durbon, Carroll Henry, 114, 124
Durbon, Lillian, 114-115, 124
"Dust Bowl," 139

E

Eagle Creek (Oregon), 107
Emergency Relief Organization, 19

F

Fechner, Robert (national CCC Director, 1933-1939), *22*, 52, *134*
Ferris, John, 113
Fort George Wright Civilian Conservation Corps District, *96*
Fort Lewis Civilian Conservation Corps District, 99, 100, *102*, 107, 109, 125
Fort McPherson (Georgia), 36, 45, 76
Fort Simcoe State Park, 128-129

G

Garn, Louis, *148*
Gasper, George, *148*
George, Darryl, *148*
Gifford Pinchot National Forest, 42
Ginkgo Petrified Forest State Park, 104
Great Depression, The
    causes, 15-17
    effects, 4, 9, *14*, 18-20, 71, 94, 156
    unemployment, 18, 19, 33
Green, Jack, 103
Greenway, Wes, 5

H

Halloway, Paul, *148*
Hanson, Edmund C., 59, 77
Hard Labor Creek (Georgia), 23, 26, 29-31, 32
Hemlock Ranger Station, 108
Hill, Edwin G., (family and relatives)
    Hill, Allen (half brother), 11
    Hill, Bessie (stepmother), 11
    Hill, Carole Ann (daughter), 93
    Hill, Deuella (mother), 8, 9-10, 11
    Hill, Edwin Wayne (son), 93
    Hill, Henry (father), 4-5, 7, 8, 9, 10, 11, 82
    Hill, Howard Clayton "Boots" (brother), 2, 5, 24-25, 139, 164-165
    Hill, Ronald Edwin (son), 93

    Hill, Velma Barger (wife), *67*, 79-81, 83-85, 93
    Patrick, Elmer (cousin), 6
    Patrick, Felix (uncle), 6
    Patrick, Julian (cousin), 6, 25
    Poole, Grover (nephew), *61*
    Poole, Henriella Hill (sister), 2, 10, *61*
    Poole, William (nephew), *61*
Hill Chapel Baptist Church, 11
Hirsch, Major Ralph, 105
Hoover, Herbert (U. S. President), 18-19
"Hooverville" (Seattle), *14*
Hoyt, Ray (editor, *Happy Days*), 153
Huckleberries, *64*, *65*, 71, 72-74
    Indian rights, 73

I

Ice Cave (Skamania County), 86
Indian Heaven Wilderness, 70

J

Jenkins, Tim, 4
Jewsberry, Harry, *148*
Johnson, "Big Foot," *62*, 92
Jordon, Buck, 79

K

Klingensmith, Oliver, *148*

L

Lander, Pat H., 167
Langfield, K. C., 168
Lawrence, Paul A., 105
Leach, Nolan "Shack-Pole," 4
Leavy, Charles H. (U. S. Representative), 115
Lewis and Clark State Park, 115
Lewis River, 89, 90, 92
    East Fork of the Lewis River, 42, 46, 48, *61*, 85
Lewiston Civilian Conservation Corps District, *96*
Local Experienced Men (LEM's), 43, 54, 109, 127, 128
Lueck, Lieutenant Robert, 117

M

McDermott, "Cotton," 85
McDonaghie, James R., *148*
McEntee, James (national CCC Director, 1940-1942), *134, 149*
McGill, Paul, 166
McKay, Alex, 77, 168
McReynolds, J. D., 98-99, 160-161
Marshall, Brigadier General George C., 43
Martin, Clarence (Washington Governor), 127
Martin, H. C., *66*
Martin, Jack, *61*
Martin, Ruth H., 167
Metaline Falls, 109
Moran, Robert (industrialist/philanthropist), 123
Moran State Park, 123
Mortimer, Pap, *148*
Mosley, General George Van Horn, 37
Mt. Adams, 12, *65*, 70, 73, 76, 110, 129
Mt. Constitution, 125, 126, *147*
Mt. Hood, 132-133, 168
Mt. Rainier, 101, 112
Mt. Rainier National Park, 110, 112, 115
Mt. St. Helens, 12, *34, 63*, 89, 91, 93

N

Naches Ranger Station, 100
Naches River, 99, 100, 127, *146*, 156
National Association of Civilian Conservation Corps Alumni
    Everett Chapter #78, 114
    NACCCA, 123, 142-143
    Tri-Cities Chapter #48, 154
    Yakima Valley Chapter #39, 94, 162
Nehr, Charles, 48
Nile Creek, 99
Nissely, Harold, *148*
Niver, Charles, 84
North Fork of Ahtanum Creek, 117, 119
Nowlin, William S., 115
    letter, 115-117

O

Odom, Archie, 166
Ohanapecosh River, 115, 117
Olney, Orville, 129-130

P

Palmer, Frank, 131
Peterson, Ole, 92-93
Peterson, Vernon, 111
Pimentel, Lieutenant Merrill, 117
Pinchot, Gifford (Chief Forester, U. S. Forest Service), 42
"Popovich," *148*

R

Randle Ranger District, 111
Read, Lieutenant W. E., 43, 56
Redfish Lake (Idaho), *151*
Reidinger, Joe, *148*
Reynolds, Stan, *148*
Roosevelt, Franklin D. (U. S. President), 20, *22*, 52, 133, 141
"Roosevelt's Tree Army" (Civilian Conservation Corps), 138
Ropp, Emma, 80
Rust, David, 103
Rutledge (Georgia), 11, 23, 26

S

StJohn, Audley "A. G.," 58-59, 79, 80, *148, 149*, 165-168
Schaefer, Gilbert, 126
Schaffhauser, Joseph F., Sr., 157-159
Schaffner, Myer, 159-160
Sherry, Leonard, 103
Shiloh Baptist Church (Georgia), 7-9
Silver Star Mountain, 44, 46-47, 55, *62*
Skykomish blaze, 128
Smith, Robert, 109
Snoqualmie River, 121, 122
Snyder, Victor, 54-58, 156-157
Soil Conservation Service, 44, *96*, 117, 119, 120, *149, 151*
"Soil Soldiers" (Civilian Conservation Corps), *96*
Spokane Indian Reservation, 128
Sprague, Kenneth, 103, *148*
"Spud Hill" fire, 128

Stock Market Crash, 1, 17
Storey, Ellsworth (architect), 126, *147*
Sunset Falls, 42, 46, 54, *61*

T

Tate, Ernie, *148*
Teed, Ryle, 168
Tieton River, 127
Tillamook burn, 130-132
Timberline Lodge (Oregon), 132-133
Trout Creek Dam, 108, *146*
Twin Buttes, 11, 44, 57, *63, 64,* 70
Twin Buttes Lookout, *63*
Twiss, S. N., 119-120

U

U. S. Forest Service, 42, 76, 83, 86, 109, 121, 132, 141, 154, 159

V

Vancouver, 36, 39, 54, 59, 91, 106
Vancouver Barracks Civilian Conservation Corps District, 40, *41,* 42-43, 45, 54, 132, 157, 162
Von Spacher, Jim, 118-119

W

Walla Walla Treaty, 73
Waring, Major C. T., 168
Warm Springs Indian Reservation, 73, 128
Washington State Parks and Recreation Commission, 114, 129, 141
West, William C., *148,* 166
White, Captain John G., 43, 56
Whitehorse peak, *147*
Whitfield, "Leather Head," 50
"Widow-makers," 42, 159
Wildlife, 30, 39, 104, 112, 120, 124
Willard blaze, 81-83
Wind River Experiment Station, 108
Works Progress Administration (WPA), 104, 132
World War I (1914-1918), 15-16, 17, 18-19
World War II (1939-1945), 126, 136-138, 153, 160-165, 168

Y

Yacolt burn, 42, 54, 58, *60*
Yakima Indian Reservation, 73, 84, 115, 128-130

Z

Ziegler, Lieutenant Everett F., 168